HELPING OTHERS

Robert J. Wicks

Ways of Listening,
Sharing and
Counselling

HELPING OTHERS

Robert J. Wicks

Ways of Listening, Sharing and Counselling

A CONDOR BOOK

SOUVENIR PRESS (E & A) LTD.

First published in the USA by
Chilton Book Company
Reissued 1982 by Gardner Press, Inc., New York

First British edition published 1994 by
Souvenir Press (Educational & Academic) Ltd,
43 Great Russell Street, London WC1B 3PA

ISBN 0 285 63159 4

Printed in Great Britain by
The Guernsey Press Co. Ltd, Guernsey, Channel Islands

For Michaele, naturally

Writing *Helping Others* was an adventure for me. Developing a brief book which would serve to bring important counseling principles into the home and office was an exciting challenge. Happily, I had someone to share the process of this book's development with me— my wife and "personal counselor," Michaele. In addition to providing inspiration, support, and encouragement, she suggested changes, provided editing, and gave me detailed feedback at each stage of the work. So, in dedicating this book, I'm pleased to acknowledge her contributions and her patience.

Contents

Chapter 1 You *Can* Help   1

Chapter 2 How to Listen   6

               Anxiety: A Communication Block   7
               Overcoming the Savior Complex   9
               Enduring Silence   10
               Recognizing Nonverbal Signs in Others   13
               Recognizing Our Own Nonverbal Signs   17

Chapter 3 Getting Information   21

               Conversation with a Goal   21
               Humility: A Valuable Asset   24
               The Art of Questioning   25
               Focusing Your Questions   29
               The Level of the Question   33
               Getting the Complaint in Detail   34
               Answering Questions with Questions   37
               Dealing with Unsatisfactory Responses   41
               Transitions between Topics   41

Chapter 4 Tuning In to Others   44

               Adopting the Other's Frame of Reference   44
               Criticizing Our Reactions   47

A Distorted View of the Helper 50
Defensive Styles 51
False Courage or Denial 52
Childlike Behavior 54
Hostility and Depression 56
Evasion 58

Chapter 5   The Goals of Counseling 61

Exploring Feelings 62
Focusing on Assets 67
Clarifying Issues 69
Opening Up Alternatives 75

Chapter 6   Stages of the Interview: A Summary 82

Initial Opening 82
Unburdening and Looking for Key Clues 83
Follow-Up 84
Brainstorming 86
Tying It Up 87

Chapter 7   Some Counseling Guidelines 89

Evaluating the Session 89
Pacing 93
Dealing with Specifics 95
Pointing Out Behaviors 96
Questioning Generalizations 97
Giving Feedback 99
Showing Acceptance 100
Evaluating First, Changing Second 101
Being Patient 102

Chapter 8   Common Problems: Depression, Anxiety,
and Stress 104

Who Gets Depressed? 105
Signs of Depression 107
Physical Causes of Depression 109
Dealing with Helplessness 110
Depression and Anger 117
Anxiety in Daily Life 121

	Causes of Anxiety Problems	123
	Coping with Anxiety	124
	Counseling Anxious People	125
	Causes of Stress	128
	Handling Stress	128

Chapter 9   Handling a Crisis   133

	Self-Injurious Behavior	134
	Taking Action with the Suicidal	136
	Drug Abuse Emergencies	138
	Alcohol Abuse	138
	Hallucinogens and the Bad Trip	141
	Opiate Overdose	142
	Amphetamine Abuse	143
	Bizarre Behavior	144
	The Assault Victim	146
	The Rape Victim	148
	Crisis Intervention	150
	Divorce—An Illustration of Crisis Intervention	152

Chapter 10   Self-Help and Pop-Psychology Books   156

	The Appeal of Popular Psychology Books	157
	Their Limitations	160
	Their Advantages	164
	Selecting, Using, and Recommending Them	166

Chapter 11   Obtaining Professional Help   169

	Determining the Need	169
	How to Suggest Professional Help	176
	The Mental Health Evaluation	179
	Ground Rules of Therapy	180
	Types of Mental Health Workers	182
	Types of Treatment	184
	Consumerism	186

Chapter 12   Common Questions about Helping Others   189

Index   204

Chapter 1

You *Can* Help

Helplessness is always a distressing feeling, and in our era of progress and achievement, this feeling can be even more disconcerting. After all, we have been taught that with education and training—and a lot of motivation—almost anything is possible. Nevertheless, there have surely been occasions in your life when someone close (a child, parent, spouse, employee, friend) has reached out to you because they have been unable to cope. In response to their expression of confusion, misery, or anxiety, you might have tried to give good advice, but may also have felt uncomfortable and ill equipped to be of any real assistance.

This awkward feeling of not knowing how to help a friend is widely experienced—yet it need not be. Most of us have healthy personalities and effective interpersonal styles. All we need is guidance in making the most effective use of ourselves and what we already know about people. The goal of *Helping Others* is to offer some of this guidance.

Today there is a plethora of aids for almost every problem, how-to manuals that range from macrame and vegetable growing to building your own vacation home and saving your marriage. Today, too, the ranks of professional counselors and therapists have swollen tremendously, as has the number of books on self-help and enlightenment, pop-psychology, and meditation.

Yet there is little written on how we can help our family, friends, neighbors, and business colleagues when they are feeling anxious or depressed. Considering how far we've progressed in public education in other areas, one can't help wonder why there isn't more information available on helpful counseling for our daily use.

One businessman said many of his co-workers come to him for support. Although he believed he could help them, he expressed dismay at the lack of down-to-earth books available to help him to be more efficient.

A mother once exclaimed to me, "I have a depressed neighbor. She comes to me and I don't know what to say to her. Is there anything I can do besides merely hearing her out and eventually saying, 'Go seek help elsewhere?' "

And what about our families? Constantly we must deal with an angry child, a distant adolescent, or a temporarily upset spouse. Isn't there something we can learn about interviewing and counseling to help us help them?

To keep basic, practical mental health information from people not in the mental health field is elitist, pedantic, and in some crisis situations even dangerous. In a society in which alienation and isolation are becoming more and more prevalent, helping other people reach out more effectively to their family, friends, and business acquaintances is not merely a desirable undertaking—it's an essential, humane pursuit.

Recent presidential commissions in the United States have recognized the magnitude of mental health problems in the nation; no age, race, sex, ethnic, religious, or socioeconomic group is exempt. As families become smaller, cities and businesses become larger, schools begin numbering us, and the demand for job mobility increases, our support systems shrink. When we get depressed, we find there's no one to hear us cry; when we get angry, there are few people to turn to who will let us scream out. And when we feel the stress of modern existence and the pain of troubled personal relations, we often look in vain for that special someone who will hear us out.

Helping Others, then, is written as a partial antidote to the isolation and potential alienation of people in a world that is moving too fast and, in the process, rapidly discouraging people from fulfilling their human responsibilities to each other. It is a mental health first-aid book enabling us to assist others who are experiencing some emotional distress.

Such a book is certainly in keeping with recent developments in preventive psychiatry and community psychology. The establishment of local community mental health clinics and the hiring of competent, caring paraprofessionals with a bachelor's degree or less is based on the well-founded belief that professionals cannot *and need not* do it alone.

There's nothing wrong with reaching out for help to a professional. In many instances they are needed as a supportive, objective helper. In our age of specialization, though, there seems to be an increasing trend to use hotlines, psychotherapists, counselors, and psychopharmacologic drugs instead of first turning to family and friends. Yet often, particularly in a minor crisis, colleagues, family, or friends could have provided the needed help.

Many people wouldn't and probably shouldn't go to a psychologist to discuss a small problem. Still others feel more at home initially discussing big problems with someone they know before seeking professional help. And everyone recognizes the importance of dealing with problems before they get out of hand. Even in those cases where professional help is necessary, the presence of other supportive relations can help move the process along more quickly. We need each other if we are to be healthy and happy.

If we have flexible, supportive friends who are willing to listen, then we are more apt to challenge our unproductive patterns of dealing with the world. If we have people who will listen to us and give us feedback without malice, the decisions we make to risk change, to be more accepting of ourselves, to become more productively assertive with others, become easier and more feasible.

It doesn't have to be a catastrophe for us to utilize helping techniques. Situations arise daily in which we meet others who need our assistance. Most of us can be of use in such instances. All we need is a basic knowledge of helping methods to direct and expand our natural talents.

Helping Others tries to do this. It is a nontechnical, easy-to-read, compact volume on interviewing and counseling. The goal of this book is to help you learn how you can:

Play an active, helping role with family, friends, and ac-
    quaintances
Listen actively
Be supportive
Help problem-solve
Understand more fully the common problems of depression,
    anxiety, and stress
Deal with mental health emergencies
Better evaluate self-help literature
Know when and how to help others seek professional help

This book is based on a simple philosophy: to really foster community health we must equip today's intelligent adult population with some basic mental health information that will help them better understand themselves as well as extend and improve their ability to work with others. This premise doesn't deny the need for professionals or minimize the role they play. Serious mental health problems are put in their proper perspective and one of the chapters in this book explains how to determine whether someone can use professional assistance and how such a referral can be made in an effective, logical fashion.

Helping Others provides practical information on how to better interact with others as an empathetic, helpful person on a day-to-day basis. This book does not make light of emotional distress or provide a cute, superficial view of personal difficulties. Nor is this book designed to turn the reader into a psychologist. Instead, it is designed to enhance personal talents which most of us already possess and are required to use every day.

Chapter **2**

How to Listen

During the course of a day people hear many sounds, but only *listen* to a few. Hearing is an easy, passive process. Listening requires energy, motivation, and patience.

Trying to make sense of the numerous facts and issues contained in every communication is extremely difficult. That's why when another person bombards us with a multitude of thoughts, problems, and emotions, we often respond by becoming lazy, anxious, or disinterested. As this happens we lower our attention threshold, turn our mind to other thoughts, and put on our "Oh yes, of course I'm interested" facial mask.

Embarrassingly, we sometimes get caught. But, more importantly, we have missed an opportunity to share a significant experience with another person. This is a shame, and it is one of the reasons why so many people turn to professionals for help. It is also why many of us turn to alcohol, drugs, fantasy, or decide to turn off life completely. If no one bothers to take the time out to listen to us (no matter how many people are physically present in our environment), the usual ensuing feeling is *loneliness*. And the simple fact is being alone can be scary.

6

Children in trouble often tell of being alienated from their own families at the very time when they most need their help:

"I tried to talk to my parents about sex but they wouldn't hear of it. Each time I brought up the issue of birth control, they would respond by saying, 'Are you sleeping around, Robin? If we find out that you are, you're going to be in a good deal of trouble! I don't know where you get all of these questions, but I'm sure it's those sluts you hang around with after school.' So I just stopped bringing it up."

"So, you found out about sex from . . . ?"

"Well, I got tired of being harassed by my parents, so I asked my 'slutty friends.' And they told me to take the pill if I was going to do something."

"And?"

"Well, how was I to know you were supposed to take it every day? I felt stupid enough asking them . . . They laughed at me as it was. And when Mary got some, there were no instructions. So I just took them anytime Billy and I would sleep together. So when I found out I was pregnant I couldn't figure out what I had done wrong. . . ."

"How did your parents react?"

"They went wild, called me everything in the book, and— you're not going to believe this—when they calmed down, my mother asked me, 'How come you didn't come to us sooner?'"

Why had Robin's parents closed the lines of communication? Surely not out of malice, but probably out of anxiety.

ANXIETY: A COMMUNICATION BLOCK

Anxiety is one of the leading blocks to communication. It can affect both the person listening and the person seeking assistance.

The distressed person can experience a high degree of anxiety just by telling his/her story, no matter how motivated this person may be to share the burden. Even when the two people involved know each other, such anxiety may be present.

"But I thought you said your neighbor was usually pretty sympathetic; yet you held back quite a bit when you told her about your husband's health. . . ."

"I started to tell her. I started to tell her each time I went over there, but . . . well, I just couldn't get it out. I was afraid she wouldn't understand, that she would think I didn't care about my husband and his feelings if I spent time going into how *I* felt and how his problems upset me."

In listening to someone relate a problem, therefore, we must realize and accept that they may be anxious. It's a natural reaction since we're all concerned with how we come across and are received.

A similar nervousness may also exist in the person who is the helper. One popular quote still heard in psychotherapy seminars is, "It's all right if one of the persons in the therapist's office is anxious—as long as it isn't the therapist." Accordingly, much time is spent by trainees in analyzing those things which might make the novice psychologist, clinical social worker, or psychiatrist nervous when dealing with a patient.

Probably the most common cause of anxiety in counselors is the fear of saying or doing something wrong. The feeling is, "If I don't say something, he'll think I don't understand; and if I do say something, he'll know it for sure!" Anxiety and the fear of saying the wrong thing are often tied to one or more of three faults in relating: (1) the "savior complex," (2) inability to endure silence, and (3) failure to recognize nonverbal signs.

These faults are not the special errors of therapists—they are the basis of much of the hesitancy we all have in discussing sensitive issues with others who come to us for help. The same factors that make professional therapists shy away from working with *certain* patients in *particular* circumstances make most people so anxious they wish to wash their hands of the role of "helpful listener."

OVERCOMING THE SAVIOR COMPLEX

Homo sapiens is distinguished from other species in the animal kingdom by a number of characteristics. While a positive one is our sense of humor, a negative one surely is our tendency to play at being omnipotent in dealing with others.

Humility is a rare, special trait among human beings; pomposity and arrogance, unfortunately, are less rare. That's why constructive feedback from family, friends, and peers is necessary if our estimation of ourselves is to retain some sort of basis in reality. Many "self-help" or "pop-psychology" authors might disagree with this point of view. They would say, "You should be more assertive! Say no to others! Get what's coming to you! You're not pompous, they are!" However, this is far from true. Even in the case of shy persons, it is their self-centeredness that sometimes gets them into trouble.

Shy people are used as an example here because they seem, by virtue of their very diffident behavior, to be the complete antithesis of pomposity. By looking more deeply, though, we can see that this is not completely true. If shy people weren't so convinced that *everyone* was looking at them when they walked into a room and that *everyone* would notice if they made a mistake in a conversation or social interaction, they would be more active and loquacious. In this sense they have an inflated view of themselves and of the size of the impact they make on others.

Now, if shy people have problems with inflated self-images, how about us outgoing souls? Moreover, if anything inflates the ego, it is when one of our peers comes to us with a problem or to vent feelings of frustration. The first thought striking many of us is, "My goodness, he's come to *me* for help. He must think I'm quite knowledgeable. Isn't that great."

Yet that thought barely gets a chance to brighten up our self-image before fear overtakes us with the dispiriting question, "What can I do for this person?" The implicit thought being, "Boy, is he going to be disappointed." Or, "Am I going to look bad!"

Then, with this negative feeling thoroughly imbedded, we quite naturally do either of two inappropriate things. Either we try to beg off by assuming the attitude of, "After all, what can we possibly do to help?" Or else we put on our "savior" mantle and try to heal the other person by offering advice and wise words which are designed to "lift the spirit" or be the perfect solution to his or her problem.

In both instances the person who is seeking help loses because they are either rejected or smothered with golden and often useless words of wisdom. We, the designated helpers, also lose when we leave the situation feeling frustrated because our help "didn't do the trick" or feeling guilty because we neglected to offer help at all.

This is a truly unfortunate situation when it occurs because, with a little awareness of ourselves and others, this frustrating outcome is normally unnecessary and avoidable. In reality, when someone comes to us for aid, they are usually only asking us to be a supportive and good listener. Having someone who will listen without judging, ignoring, or providing nicely pack-aged cures is in itself a great joy.

The value I place on listening may sound like an exaggeration, but it isn't. Try to recall a special situation when you just wanted someone to listen and *try* to appreciate the difficulties you were encountering. Finding the right person to fill such a role was probably very difficult, if not impossible.

ENDURING SILENCE

People in general have great difficulty dealing with silence, especially their own—which means a good listener is a rarity.

Being silent isn't easy. As a matter or fact, it's actually discouraged in modern society.

Our cars are not complete without radios, tape decks, or both. Our homes are filled with the sounds of television and stereos; and at a party we are considered quite the person if we can pick up the ball when there is a lull in the verbal action. Even in contemporary religious services sounds abound: we are either preached or sung to, or are busy doing the same ourselves as part of the congregation. Quiet meditation is becoming a thing of the past.

Therefore, for many people remaining silent is not easy. Today's societal conditioning militates against it. The value of being silent is almost obscured now in our action-oriented times.

The feeling is unless we are *doing* something, we are useless. Unfortunately, this fits in with the "savior complex," which dictates that we should rescue those asking to share a problem with us. The negative result is we fail to be silent with someone who comes to us feeling a bit down, distressed, or frustrated.

This is sad because they want us to listen. They want to unburden themselves. They want to open up and share their thoughts. This process is impossible if they are only met with talk, talk, and more talk.

A neighbor may say, "I really feel down, I don't know what to do"—and then remain silent. A friend may say the following before lapsing into silence, "My daughter is really getting the best of me." Or a family member may say, "Grandpa is not fair to me. I'm tired of listening to it"—with a long pause after the statement.

In such instances, it may not seem that the person is going to follow with an elaboration, but that's just what is needed if the listener is to be of some help. Accordingly, when people start with statements like the ones made above, the listener has two natural choices: either to remain silent, or to indicate briefly to the other person to continue. ("You've been feeling down lately . . . ? What's been happening with your daughter? What's Grandpa been doing?")

Once this encouragement has been given to the person, remaining silent and waiting for the person to elaborate is usually a safe and appropriate technique. When people are ready to open up, they will. Occasionally further prompting is necessary, but this is rare. It's usually a mistake not to religiously practice patience and perseverence. Often it is the *listener's* difficulty with silence that prompts giving further encouragement to speak, rather than the actual necessity of giving such encouragement.

After the person has begun, we may also encounter periods of silence. This can occur for any number of reasons. It may be that the individual is thinking about what to say next, he's angry, confused, embarrassed, or is waiting to see our reaction.

At such a time, unless it is a natural break and it really is time to say something, waiting is best. Waiting isn't easy, even for the experienced listener. As was indicated, due to the habit of responding in conversation and our general discomfort with silence, it is quite natural to feel under great pressure to speak up when someone else stops.

Holding back can have great benefits, though. By not responding, a vacuum is set up within which the person can think, have the opportunity to continue, change the topic, vent emotions, or just enjoy the comfort of another person's presence. By controlling ourselves we give them the freedom to express themselves.

To illustrate this, try an experiment. In a normal conversational setting, instead of being talkative, try using a "quiet approach." When someone is talking, instead of breaking in if you have a question, as you normally do, wait and remain silent. See what happens.

I always find it amazing when I hold myself back from interrupting someone with a question, or when I let a silent space go by without being the one to take control and fill it. The other person often says something which sheds new light on his or her feelings or concerns about an issue.

One of the other reasons people have a hard time keeping

silent during another person's narrative is, as I've said, they feel they're not accomplishing anything. After all, what can helpers accomplish if they merely listen?. This may be true if we were speaking about passive listening or the simple act of hearing the message the other person is trying to convey. However, in the helping process we employ "active listening."

Active listening is not just patiently keeping our mouth shut until the opportunity arises to break in and share our words of wisdom. Rather, it is a process in which we are trying to put together the whole message the person is sending. It is a method of taking what the person is saying to us now and trying to fit it into the pattern of what they have been trying to convey the whole time they've been with us.

If we just listen in a passive way, and spend this time trying to figure out something terribly bright to say when we get the chance, much will be missed. Thus, ironically, when we do get any opportunity to provide our pearls of wisdom, we probably will say something which misses the mark by a mile.

Paul Williams, the composer and singer, had on the back of one of his earlier albums, "There are those who listen, and those who wait to talk. This album is dedicated to the listeners." One could paraphrase this in reference to counselors—be they "professionals" or not. "There are those who actively listen, and those who merely hear. Counseling is done by the real listeners."

RECOGNIZING NONVERBAL SIGNS IN OTHERS

When listening is used in the counseling arena, it's defined in a very broad sense. It doesn't just refer to the use of the ears. It pertains to the eyes as well. Both senses must be used if enough information is to be sent to the brain. This is so the listener can distinguish between the *manifest content* of what the person is conveying, and the *total content* of the message being sent.

By manifest content I mean the information contained in what a person says—that is, the meaning conveyed by the words alone. By total content I'm referring to the combined verbal and nonverbal message communicated by the person. This difference is quite important. Too often the message a person verbalizes is accepted at face value. They say they're sad and we sympathize; they indicate they're happy and we rejoice. We take what people say as being simple, straightforward, and understandable. In doing this we are almost denying the complexity of the human being. The nuances in the person's speech and the subtleties of human nature are being ignored.

It's true that when some people tell us they are happy, they are indeed quite happy. And the same goes for sadness, or any other valued emotion. The problem arises when we accept the major part of their message but don't take the energy to see if any contradictory points are being expressed. The richness of human feelings is expressed in the nuances and minor paradoxes which arise when we probe further into what the person is trying to communicate.

For example, someone who has admitted a past problem with drinking too much may quickly add that he or she seems to have it under control now, but say it in a halting voice. If we ignore the dissonant note reflected in the manner of speech, much will be lost from the communication.

Probably the primary reason we miss parts of someone's communication which may modify its meaning is our lack of motivation to pursue messages which puzzle us, or our lack of understanding of the nonverbal elements of communication. Paradoxically, this lack of understanding may in part be due to the heightened attention nonverbal communication has recently been given—and the subsequent discrediting of "body language."

Though there are a number of good books on nonverbal communication, in many instances the whole business has been overplayed. There are books upon books to tell us how much is revealed by the way one leg crosses over another, or how to tell another person's strong feelings for us by the way the individual is holding himself. In such instances, nonverbal communication and its understanding have been packaged in such a way as to make people believe it can be used to control others.

This is a shame. What this kind of overplaying has done in some instances is to discredit the basic procedure of tuning in on nonverbal signs. In other instances it has made people believe they need to take a course or memorize a three-hundred-page book if they are to utilize this communicative approach.

I encourage a commonsense approach to nonverbal communication. Take note of the person's body while you're listening to his or her voice; listen both to *what* is being said as well as to *how* it is being said. Look at the face. Do the expressions match the person's verbal message, or is something awry? How about the general carriage of the individual? Is she tense? Does he look relaxed? How do emotions affect the way a person speaks? Is the person slurring the words, speaking very rapidly or lethargically? What's the tone in the person's voice? Is it edgy? Sad? Angry?

All of these kinds of things can help in bridging the gap between the spoken words and the total content of the message. Sometimes it is easy to do and sometimes it's a bit more elusive and difficult to track, but in either case, it's worth spending the energy following up.

Some nonverbal cues are easy to spot and bring to the person's attention. If someone is very happy in their demeanor while they're saying they're really down, it's easy to note and comment on. "Gee, you say you're down, but you're smiling and your voice sounds pretty bubbly!"

Or take an incident we've no doubt all encountered. A person indicates he or she is not angry verbally, but a flushed face seems to say otherwise. "Well I know you say it doesn't trouble you, but your face is red and you do seem upset." To the above statement the person may respond, "Well, it gets me angry when people say I'm getting upset; if I wasn't upset before, it gets me going." To that it's sometimes good to follow up by saying, "How come people get to you in that way? There must be a reason."

In many instances, though, the nonverbal cues are a bit more subtle. When this is so, there is a danger of missing them. Consequently, as active listeners, we must try to absorb the verbal message and also try to keep alert to body signs and changes.

Missing the signs, particularly when they are subtle, is not the only danger. Misinterpreting them is another. For example, when we see an expression on someone's face it is often hard to interpret what is going on in his or her mind. In these instances it would be a mistake to make someone else's nonverbal sign fit our own interpretation. Not only can we be mistaken, but also the person hearing our guess may become angry or resistant (and with good reason) or may actually agree with us even though our guess was wrong.

Many people agree when they are vulnerable even if they don't really believe what was said. They go along with us for a number of reasons. They may fear rejection, be confused and see agreeing as a way out, or possibly as a way to avoid looking into themselves for the answer. Whatever the reason, though, premature interpretation is unnecessary and usually harmful. At the very least it's not helpful. Moreover, remember when we do this we are asking them to go along with our "savior complex"—for we are trying to show we can read their minds.

So, what to do with a questionable nonverbal cue? The most neutral way of communicating our observation is to just point out the nonverbal sign and ask them what it means. In this way, the door is being opened. They are being asked to take the responsibility to help look at the meaning behind it.

For instance, if a man is reporting how happy he is about getting a new job, but there seems to be a hesitancy in his voice or a flicker of some kind of expression that doesn't match the mood exactly, this could be pointed out. "You seem really happy, but there's a sound in your voice (or you just had an expression on your face) that . . .?" (The comment is left unfinished on purpose to see what happens.)

To this statement the person may respond in a number of ways:

"Well, it's funny you should pick it up, but I am concerned about the duties in the new job even if it is a promotion I've always wanted."

Or, "You mean you think I'm not totally happy about the job?"

Or, "I'm not sure what you're referring to. . . ."

If the person answers in the first way, nothing more need be done. In the second and third responses, something additional needs to be said to prompt further examination of the nonverbal sign. So, the following noncommittal comment might be added: "When you were talking about some of the job's duties, your voice sounded different (or you had this look on your face); I don't have any idea what it meant, but it did confuse me and I wondered what you were thinking?"

This further push might get the person to examine the cause for the nonverbal sign. If this happens, fine. If he still seems unwilling or unable to talk about it, just drop the topic and make no more of it. This will leave him with a possible doubt, but not with the pressure of our interpretation to contend with.

One interesting thing might also happen. Later on, if elements do come up which don't fit in exactly with what the person has been saying (if, say, the person does discover a doubt about a decision that seemed completely sound), he may come back to the time when you pointed out the nonverbal sign. Then a clarification of what might have been going on at the earlier time may be broached.

RECOGNIZING OUR OWN NONVERBAL SIGNS

Up to this point we have been discussing nonverbal communication by the person coming for help. Since the interaction involves at least two people, some attention needs to be given to the listener's nonverbal communications to the person asking for aid.

In the case of even the most experienced interviewer and

counselor, there is a tendency to forget that just as the listener can be a sharp observer, so can the person coming for help. Some interviewers feel their training gives them a special edge. An outgrowth of this is they almost come to believe they are in a plastic bubble through which no one can observe their expressions or nonverbal gestures.

This, of course, is far from the reality of things. The truth of the matter is the counselee may be *more* observant than the counselor. The person opening up and telling a sensitive story or a personal tale is apt to be extremely alert to how his presentation is being received. In fact, he may have waited all day just to get together with you to share the material. On the other hand, you may have been busy all day interacting with people at work and at home and may not be especially sensitive to every detail of the conversation.

The person coming for help may be extremely sensitive to how he or she is being received. So it is very necessary for us to be aware of the nonverbal communications we send, whether they be very blatant or almost imperceptible. This awareness is especially important so we can better judge how our own expressions might affect the interaction.

The illustration of this which comes to mind occurred when I first started interviewing as a profession. It was in a criminal justice setting, and my job was to conduct intake interviews in a jail. What this entailed was trying to get basic information on a new confinee's background, crime, and personality so we could ensure they would be placed in the proper program within the institution.

On one particular morning a young, slightly built sixteen-year-old was led over to me. I asked him to sit down and began asking him a number of questions. (My goal at this point in my interviewing career was to fill in the blanks on the form the prison administration gave me. As is the case with many insecure, new interviewers, I was more interested in data than in people and their feelings.)

When I reached the section of the questionnaire devoted to a description of the crime (without having had any snags in the interaction to this point), I casually asked, "How come you're in jail?"

When he replied, "I shot my grandmother," I gave him a facial expression that said unequivocally, "You did what!!!" In effect, nonverbally I was telling him, "I could understand how you might assault your brother, fight with your mother, or rob your father, but nobody, *nobody* shoots their grandmother . . .!"

This blatant early rejection of him naturally didn't go unnoticed. From that point on in the session he became quiet and his answers were brief. After several minutes, I realized the impact of my judgmental reaction. If any progress was to be made, I would have to do something to correct for my mistake. I decided to confront the issue directly.

"When you mentioned you shot your grandmother earlier, it surprised me and I reacted without thinking. I imagine other people have responded similarly, but that's no excuse. You see, I—like possibly others—didn't even stop to hear what you had to say about how this came about. I cut you off. How did you feel when I did that?

The youth spent several minutes speaking about how he met the same response in others who had prejudged him and that it made him angry and sad. When he completed describing his response, I went on to say, "Well, if I responded to you like everyone else, it's no wonder you wouldn't want to give me a fuller picture of what happened. What did happen anyway?"

At that juncture, I was lucky. He had aired enough of his feelings. He also seemed to feel that, although I was initially prejudiced in my view, I earnestly was interested in hearing his side to the story. So, with my question, he was prompted to continue and we made some progress. The lines of communication were opened again.

The mistakes we make as listeners are not always so blatant (thank goodness!). Likewise, sometimes it's not possible to correct for it at the time. The important factor, though, is that we keep aware of as much of our nonverbal communication as possible. The more we are in touch with how we're coming across, the greater our chances are of knowing how we really feel about certain topics. If we tend to be more expressive—either positively or negatively—the probability is that we have some strong feelings in this area. And if we can become alert to these nonverbal expressions, we can work better to deal with the emotions and concerns they represent.

For example, suppose when someone speaks of drugs, sex, or family violence, it produces strong reactions which are, naturally, facially expressed. In such a case, it would be hard to seem objective when listening to someone discuss problems touching on one of these issues.

Monitoring our own nonverbal communications can be an invaluable asset in helping us learn about ourselves as we work to help others. It makes us aware of our own feelings. It lets us know when we have inadvertently or purposefully sent a message that we feel a certain way about what the other is telling us (and, in turn, have certain feelings about that person). And it helps us to control the way we come across when we want to hear someone out without imposing our biases upon him while he is relating his position or plight.

Listening to others, then, is a very active, often complex process. It involves attending to those topics which make us anxious, the fear we have of being trapped into an "omnipotent" role of healer, the discomfort we have with remaining silent, and the need to be cognizant of nonverbal signs in others and ourselves. Attending to these things, though, makes it possible for us to become a more empathetic, accepting person.

Active, helpful listening is not an easy process. Rather, it is a process which takes practice and aptitude to undertake effectively. Certainly it is a process which should not leave us with time to question whether we are "doing" enough. In listening actively, we are immersed in receiving as much as is humanly possible of the total communication being sent to us by another person.

Chapter 3

Getting Information

Knowing what another person is undergoing is naturally a prerequisite for taking some action and providing some help. One of the ways we discover the many intricate facets of a person's situation is through listening. Although a complicated process in itself, listening is only part of the total interpersonal communication approach called *interviewing*.

CONVERSATION WITH A GOAL

Many of us think of interviewing as a special process used by employment agencies, in medical settings, or possibly by newspaper reporters. In other words, interviewing is seen as a technical undertaking employed by specialists in particular fields.

More familiar to most people is the interaction called "conversation." This process is used in everyday living. It is free-floating, usually aimless, and is entered into quite naturally by most

21

of us. A conversation's goal is frequently ill-defined or quickly changed. So while conversation can be easy, it's not always productive. We can't count on finding out things during a conversation; we might, but unless we're on our toes and making an effort to elicit certain material during the encounter, nothing is guaranteed.

What people don't often realize, though, is that when they are trying to reach a goal during a conversation, they are, in fact, conducting an interview. Interviewing is actually a *purposeful conversation*, the purpose being to secure information.

Ironically, nonprofessional conversationalists who are goal oriented in their approach to others sometimes turn out to be much better interviewers than their professional counterparts. One of the reasons for this is the relatively relaxed style of the "unpaid interviewer" conducting a purposeful conversation.

Too often, employed professionals use a rigid approach and put interviewees on the defensive. They put on their "interviewer face" and use their "professional voice" to ask questions. One psychologist reported an episode that illustrates this point. He was traveling with a colleague and they had been chatting pleasantly about a variety of light happenings. Then at one point in the conversation he decided to share a problem which was bothering him.

Almost immediately after beginning his narration, he noted, "She stiffened up, her face became expressionless, and her voice formalized to ask me 'How I felt about what I was expressing.' Since it was a sad story, how did she expect me to feel? Marvelous? Having her treat me like a patient turned me off so much that I stopped talking."

In training interviewers and therapists, a favorite question of mine when I feel the trainee is getting rigid is, "What would you have said if the inverviewee wasn't a patient, but a real person?" This teasing helps workers realize the way they have distanced themselves from the people they are interviewing.

Pedantically using an authoritarian voice when interacting with a friend in trouble accomplishes nothing. It only highlights the insecurity and pomposity of the person doing the interviewing, and it can cause tension and resentment in the interviewee. When the person being dealt with is relaxed and doesn't feel on the spot, more information can be gleaned about the issue in question.

The helpful counselor tries to maintain a relaxed, personal atmosphere. He or she also avoids "playing parent" and treating the person in trouble like a child. Too often, when a helpless adult comes for assistance, people enjoy being parental and assume an authority role. This is unfortunate because it encourages an unhealthy dependence and also supports the erroneous and unpalatable tenet that coming for help is tantamount to an act of weakness.

Making someone else feel like a child is not in that person's best interest. Treating the person as an adult and his or her problem with respect will encourage expression of feelings and information (that, after all, is your goal)—and it keeps you out of the unrewarding trap of playing rescuer or parent.

An interview is a purposeful conversation which seeks to secure information. Consequently, the style of conducting it should be as natural and conversational as any daily interaction. The idea is to be goal-oriented without appearing forced in your approach.

This may seem like a difficult or tricky undertaking, but it doesn't have to be. If several things are kept in mind, the interaction should go quite smoothly. Here are some basic pointers:

1. Try to put yourself in the other person's position. How would you like a neighbor or friend to address you if you had a problem?

2. Active listening and reasonable questioning procedures, not probing, will get you the information you need.

3. Don't treat a person seeking help like a child, because that will greatly inhibit the person's problem-solving abilities. When trouble comes up, it is the adult part of the person you are appealing to and are trying to help him rediscover.

Conducting an interview or helping session is not easy, but

keeping the above points in mind should make it easier to keep the proper perspective. Above all, they should instill *humility*.

HUMILITY: A VALUABLE ASSET

Humility is knowing what's good about yourself, knowing those aspects of yourself which are not always desirable, and accepting both groups of character traits as reality. Humility is essential for working with people because it's easy to lose sight of the reality about ourselves and unthinkingly impose ourselves on the other.

At a party it's not uncommon for a psychologist or psychiatrist to be joking around and mingling in a relaxed fashion until it is revealed that she or he is in fact a "shrink" (the nickname given to a psychotherapist). After this occurs, invariably someone will laugh nervously and say in a half-joking manner, "You're not going to analyze me are you?"

This response is an example of the mystique that surrounds people in the helping profession, just as there is folklore about people in any technical or artistic field. The problem is that some mental health practitioners tend to go along with the mystique and take a lofty position in regard to themselves. The pipe-smoking, know-it-all, "all the world's a couch and I am its shrink" mentality is all too common.

The result is that instead of hearing what another person says in terms of the situation they're in (helpless and vulnerable because of a temporary loss of coping powers) some practitioners concentrate on the superior position they happen to be in by virtue of the other person's vulnerability. In other words, rather than seeing themselves as facilitators, they see themselves as healers. And instead of viewing what the person is saying as a function of the problems he or she is having, they take the comments personally.

So, if the person praises them, they revel in it and seek to encourage such comments. If the person gets angry with them, they take it as a personal rebuff and argue with the person. When this occurs, the communication stops because the therapist is concentrating on the emotion in a personal way, rather than seeing what is producing the praise or the negative onslaught.

In performing a function such as interviewing—be you a professional or not—it is essential to take a helpful stance while trying not to build up an image of yourself at the expense of the person who is relating a problem.

The goal is to see yourself in the other person's place and to know how difficult it is to admit a personal flaw, conflict, or frustration with a peer. If this can be accomplished, the person will be more easily put at ease and the information will flow in a more productive fashion.

THE ART OF QUESTIONING

As in the case of any type of interviewing, no matter how positive the stance of the interviewer, there comes a time when a question is appropriate. The problems inherent in developing and asking questions are numerous, though, and asking the right type of question is an artful pursuit—but it is a skill that can be learned, given an understanding and practice of a few basic principles.

The first of these principles is *to ask as few questions as possible*. The reason for this is that anytime one breaks in to ask a question, it interrupts the flow of communication by the person seeking help. How many times have you been in the middle of explaining something and interrupted over and over again by annoying questions? If the person had only waited a few moments, the answer would have been forthcoming. The person was just impatient or had to hear himself talk. (Caution: You can't be actively listening if you're so busy formulating questions.)

A second principle is to make your questions short, clear, and to the point. Stress or high emotions produce situations in which diminished amounts of information can be received and understood. A poorly formed question will be harder for someone distressed to interpret than might normally be the case. So a question must be clear and purposeful. Each question needs to be formulated and presented with the hope of eliciting specific data in a particular area.

Complex or compound sentences require a number of points to be addressed. This may cause confusion or result in part of the question going unanswered: "You say you haven't been feeling well and that your appetite isn't so good. How are you doing now?" (Does this question refer to the person's general health, appetite, or both?) "Oh, I think I'm getting better now." (Is his general health improving, or is he referring to both his health and appetite?)

Another element in good questioning is to decide the *type* of question the situation calls for and act accordingly. Questions can be divided into two types: *open* and *closed*. An open question is designed to get the person to deal with areas with a broad stroke. It is not a focused method of getting at specifics. It is a way of permitting the interviewee to launch out on a topic, without the cumbrances of too much pressure on the part of the interviewer.

Here are some examples of open questions:

"Tell me a bit about how you've been feeling at work."

"What are your feelings when you have to call John and tell him you won't go out with him?"

"You say Mary upsets you. What do you mean?"

"Well, what are your plans for the future?"

Open questions are not designed to tie things together. On the contrary, they are meant to open previously packaged thoughts and feelings on an issue so they can be viewed by you and the interviewee together. Since our goal is to encourage communication and freedom within the interpersonal interaction, most of our questions will be of this nature.

There are times, though, when closed questions are necessary. Usually closed questions are used when a detailed or a yes or no response is required. The time to use them normally occurs toward the end of the discussion on a topic when the interviewer is trying to tie things up in his or her mind:

"So how long did you date John?"

"Are you afraid of confronting him then?"

"Where were you when this happened to you?"

There's nothing wrong with using a closed question. A problem only occurs when it is used incorrectly, namely when the form is biased, and when the closed question is used inadvertently in place of an open one.

A biased question is a leading, closed question. This is when the person is given only one or several choices for an answer. It's a style which forces the person to choose from a limited number of responses: "Anyone who would do something like that has to be callous, right?" (One choice.) "When she did that, did you think she was being cowardly or shy?" (Two choices.)

Such leading questions corner a person. Even if they are being guided toward a correct answer, the danger is always present that they are being forced to agree with your perceptions of the matter. Moreover, children and some elderly adults, who can be quite suggestible, may agree with you even if your perceptions aren't correct.

A direct question doesn't have to be a leading one. In the first example above, the question could be phrased, "What do you think of someone who does something like that?" Or, if the person has made it evident that in his opinion the individual under discussion is in fact callous, you can phrase it accordingly: "From what you say, it sounds like you believe the person is callous."

Another problem with closed questions arises when they're used as if they were open ones. When this occurs, the results can be quite discouraging for everyone involved.

A number of years ago I was sitting in a room with a new interviewer. It was an initial contact with a despondent youth in her early twenties. The interviewer was anxious to get a good deal of information for a conference review of the case. During the ten or fifteen minutes she was with us, it seemed he had asked her hundreds of closed questions. In response she answered all of them briefly and to the point. (She was doing exactly what he had asked of her.)

Finally, when she left he was quite discouraged. He commented to me, "Whew! Was she ever uncommunicative. I asked her question upon question, and all she gave me were brief, terse replies. She must be holding something back."

His discouragement is understandable. Yet the fact remains that it wasn't the interviewee's fault. She was taking her cue from him. He started with questions to which one could only reply with short answers. She accommodated him. If he had begun by letting her tell her story and waited to zero in on areas she was vague about, the results would have been much more satisfying all around.

Another important part of the art of questioning is learning how to handle interruptions. You already know to ask as few questions as possible so *you* don't interrupt the flow of information. But what if someone or something else demands momentary attention? If an unavoidable interruption occurs during your conversation, it needs to be handled carefully. If it isn't, the person may be turned off—and with good reason.

I'm sure we've all been in situations where we were pouring out our hearts to someone and have been interrupted by a telephone call or visitor coming in to see the person we were addressing. In one instance when this happened, the person excused himself and came back to me and tried to resume by saying, "Let's see, now where were we?" Since I had been sitting with him for ten minutes telling him things that almost had me in tears, I was really upset that he hadn't remembered where we were. My feeling was, "Well if you don't remember, I guess we were nowhere!"

So as counselors, when we are interrupted from the outside, we should try to minimize the negative effect of the temporary distraction. This can be done by trying to remember the last few words said when the telephone rings or when someone interrupts. Then when you've finished quickly with whomever has intruded, you can return, excuse yourself, and say, "Let's see, you were saying _____" (noting the last several words the person had said). This demonstrates your interest in the person and gets the session back on target.

FOCUSING YOUR QUESTIONS

Your questions will be most helpful if they are infrequent, simple, purposeful, and open (unless a closed question is necessary). Furthermore, each *series* of questions should be designed to uncover not isolated facts and feelings, but a web of related factors, thoughts, and feelings that comprise a description of the problem itself and of the person's perception of it. For example, if a youth is telling us about problems in finding employment, questions regarding how he is searching for a new position, what educational background he has, what types of positions he's held in the past, and what his hopes and expectations for his future are should provide us with a better description of his situation.

Feelings and perceptions about a problem can be explored on at least three levels: personal, interpersonal, and environmental. In seeking information, we are in fact looking simultaneously at all three of these areas.

The strictly personal level is an unobservable, unique one. Our personality is responsible for the unique way we view ourselves and the world. No matter how much someone loves us, no matter how close someone is to us, no one views us exactly as we view ourselves. And, because of our special make-up and environmental history, no one views the world exactly as we do. There will be many who occasionally see us as we see ourselves; likewise, some will agree with one of our opinions of the world. But our total personal view of ourselves and the world is unique.

Therefore, one of the areas we are interested in when a person comes to us for help is the strictly personal one of how he or she feels and thinks about the current situation. The same kind of predicament can be viewed and reacted to in any number of ways. Our job is to ferret out this person's particular view and help make it more clearly known to him or her.

For instance, if your friend's twenty-year-old daughter has decided to move into an apartment in the heart of the city, there can be a number of ways this action can be seen by a mother. One of them is "She's too young! I won't let her do it."

This mother is critical in a negative way. Her feeling is that she must act in a domineering manner to protect her daughter. No thought is given to the positive possibilities of the move, or the potential failure of such an action. To open up this area so the person can look at it more fully, a number of questions might have to be asked, such as:

"Have you discussed with your daughter when you think she will be old enough to move out?"

"What do you think will happen when you put your foot down and tell her she can't leave?"

"It sounds like you're pretty upset about this. How do you feel about this whole matter?"

"What's been going on that led up to her making the decision at this time?"

In the questions above, the effort is to get the woman to look at her own feelings and thoughts, and at her resultant plans regarding the situation. It is also designed to let her see how her style of viewing and dealing with the world is having an impact on her daughter.

Another mother might view the same situation in a slightly different way. "Mary is going to move out. I must admit I don't like it . . . I guess I'm worried about her, but she has to make the move sooner or later."

This woman seems more in touch with her *own* feelings regarding her daughter's decision. She also seems less critical in a negative way. In addition, she appears to be more aware of her role and her daughter's rights. Yet there are still a number of questions which could be asked to help the woman look at her feelings and thoughts more directly:

"What kinds of things are you worried about?"

"When would you have preferred she make the move?"

"What did she say when she told you about the move?"

"You seem ambivalent about her decision. How do you feel about it?"

Naturally, the above only illustrate several types of questions which could be asked. The idea is to get the person to focus in on herself. In doing this we try to put her feelings, no matter what they are, on the table. The more she can see her fears, concerns, joys, and frustrations, the better it is for all concerned.

Also, we can and should try to support the person without supporting her actions. For example, if she says, "I know I sound silly being so upset, but I can't help it," a reply can be, "Why is it silly?"

The person may say, "Well, she has to move out sometime." At that point the response can be, "That may be true, and I think you recognize that fact, but it's still o.k. to worry. You can't deny the way you feel."

Focusing on the overlapping interpersonal area is as important as uncovering someone's inner, personal feelings. In exploring the interpersonal area, the questions posed should be directed to the style of interaction someone uses with one or more people involved in the problem being presented.

Take the following situation, for example:

"My boss said I wasn't producing enough, that I was wasting time. I asked him whether he wanted quality work or a lot of garbage. And when I told my co-worker what he said, do you know what she suggested? She actually said I spend too much time on the phone. Can you believe that? I told her she was missing the point."

This worker is obviously denying there is a problem. Instead of hearing the complaint, she is blocking the information from getting through and is taking a very defensive position. Getting through to this woman is going to be quite difficult, but a number of questions and comments may help open up the area a bit:

"What prompted your boss to talk to you about this?"

"When he started telling you what he thought, how did you feel?"

"How did he react when you told him what you thought?"

"What is of positive value in what your co-worker or boss said?"

The idea is to chip away at what's going on, not to mount a frontal attack. Once again, falling into the savior complex must be avoided at all cost. The goal is not to force the person to see the light, but rather to help shine at least a thin ray of light on the situation. By trying too hard to force the person to see a particular point or by being even the slightest bit overly direct with this type of person, a rebuff may result.

Finding out about a person's environment is also an important goal. Just as the person's inner feelings and interpersonal interactions have an impact on the outcome of a situation, environmental pressures and resources can also significantly affect the results.

Social environment is comprised of a number of factors. The family group, vocational opportunities and issues, neighborhood resources and liabilities, social networks (religious affiliations, clubs, etc.) and other outside sources of support or frustration all contribute to how a person deals with life's challenges.

In the case of the daughter leaving home to get an apartment for herself, the social environment could be explored in terms of both the mother and the daughter. As the mother spoke about both her misgivings and positive feelings about the move, a number of questions might naturally come up which could help uncover relevant patterns in the environment. With regard to the daughter, the following questions might be asked:

"What kind of neighborhood is she moving to?"

"Will she be living with a friend? Does she have friends close by?"

"What does she perceive as the advantages and disadvantages of having her own apartment?"

"Will it be easier for her to get to her job and the educational and social environments she is interested in?"

With the mother in mind, other questions might arise:

"How will your life change when your daughter moves?"

"How will the move affect other people in the family? What do they think about her getting her own place?"

THE LEVEL OF THE QUESTION

Questions must be worded in a way that the person can easily understand them. This point is especially emphasized in training mental health professionals since they sometimes have a tendency to use jargon when speaking to a patient. However, the problem is also worth mentioning to anyone in a helping role as interviewer or counselor.

The following story, which I heard several years ago, illustrates the point:

A novice plumber's assistant wrote to the National Bureau of Standards to ask if he could use hydrochloric acid to clean out drainage pipes. In response he received the following message from one of the workers: "The efficacy of hydrochloric acid is indisputable, but the corrosive residue is incompatible with metallic permanence."

Upon getting this letter, the plumber's helper sent the following note to the worker at the Bureau: "I really appreciate your help. Thank you for letting me know it's o.k. to use it."

The worker showed this reply to a colleague. His co-worker reacted by saying, "You always get carried away with the jargon; now we have to send him another note, but this time I'll write it." The letter he sent him was as follows: "We cannot assume responsibility for the production of toxic and noxious residue from hydrochloric acid and I suggest you use an alternate procedure."

This letter also secured a response from the plumber's assistant. It said something to the effect, "Yes, I know hydrochloric acid works all right. Someone else has already written to tell me about it."

Finally, the director of the National Bureau of Standards heard about the incident and decided to send the plumber's helper a final, brief, to-the-point note.

"Don't use hydrochloric acid. It eats the hell out of pipes."

To get our point across and to avoid being misunderstood we must try to be clear and direct in what we say. Otherwise we run the risk of having an additional, unwarranted communication problem to contend with in our interaction.

GETTING THE COMPLAINT IN DETAIL

Too often in counseling and interviewing, the complaint is skipped over too lightly. When the complaint has not been voiced in detail, getting bogged down in trying to give general advice, useless supportive statements, and jumping to find quick, easy solutions can result. This can only lead to frustration for the helper and possibly annoyance or feelings of futility for the troubled individual who came for help.

Consequently, getting specific details is given first priority when a problem is reported. What, when, with whom, and under what circumstances are questions which need to be answered. Without answers to them, proceeding further may be a rocky, precarious adventure.

When a fellow says he's in trouble because he feels inadequate, find out:

What does he mean by "inadequate"? Everyone uses words in a slightly different manner, so find out in detail what this person means by "inadequate" in reference to himself.

When does he feel inadequate? Don't accept "All the time" as an answer. If he says this, then ask when does he feel more inadequate than usual.

With whom does he feel inadequate? And, for that matter, with whom does he feel *less* inadequate? How does he account for the difference?

Under what specific circumstances does he feel inadequate? In other words, where is he and what kinds of things is he thinking and feeling during, before, and after the experience?

By getting the details, the helper and the troubled person can look at the issue in a problem-solving manner. This process is in itself curative. By looking at the facts, a feeling starts to emerge that "Gee, there are reasons and factors for my feelings and behavior. Maybe I can do something about it, other than sit around and worry."

Here is a brief illustration of how the reported problem of inadequacy might be dealt with:

"I don't know, Jill. Lately I just feel so behind everyone, so inadequate."

"Arlene, I don't quite know what you mean when you say 'inadequate.'"

"You know, inadequate, inadequate . . . I don't know how else to put it."

"I guess what I'm getting at is that people experience things in different ways. When I get down, for example, I feel sort of empty. Other people say when they get blue, they feel off in a corner. How would you describe it when you feel inadequate?"

"Oh. Well, I think I see what you mean, but I still don't think I can tell you. . . ."

"Just do your best."

"Well, I guess I feel sort of, well, like *less*. Yes, that's it. I feel less."

"Less?"

"Yeh, like smaller, like a little child who is awkward, stupid, and well . . . almost like my head is full of cotton because I can't seem to function smoothly."

"Can you give me an example of when you felt like that?"

"Oh, I can give you plenty of examples. I feel that way all the time now."

"Just give me an illustration that comes to mind."

"You know it's funny, I can't think of any now. (Long silence) I just can't think of any."

"Well, how about an incident that really brought the point home. One that made you say, 'Good grief! I really feel inadequate. I really feel like a small little child.'" (Note reuse of Arlene's own words.)

"That's easy!! Just at work this morning I felt that way when one of the salesmen came in and asked me for information on one of the new drugs the company is marketing. I got so nervous I fell apart. I couldn't find the damn file, much less the handout he needed. Finally, my boss came in and found it immediately. I felt like such a jerk."

"Do you feel that way only with the sales personnel?"

"No. That's just it. I also feel it with the product managers and the advertising execs as well."

"How about your immediate boss?"

"No, not really. Sometimes I guess."

"When?"

"Well once when she asked me to take her place while she was temporarily taking over her boss's job at a convention in Boston. I thought I was going to pieces. The thing that surprised me is I always thought I could do her job. It's not that hard, you know."

"Did you have ample time to prepare for the position?"

"No, that's just it. She burst in one day and said, 'Tomorrow we have to go to Boston and John—her boss—can't make it. So, I'll have to fill in for him and you'll have to take over for me.' I was flabbergasted."

"If you had more time, do you think you could have done it?"

"Not well."

"Better than you did?"

"Well, I guess so. Yes."

"How about if the sales rep had called before coming over and said he would be picking up the info on the new drug in a half hour; do you think you could have found it?"

"Oh, sure. But that's silly. I shouldn't have gotten so upset just because he came in without warning."

"Well maybe you're right. But the issue is, you don't *always* feel and function inadequately."

"So, big deal."

"It is a big deal. The more you can find out about when and how you start to feel inadequate, the more you can see what's causing it and how to handle it. At the very least now, you can see that when you're caught off guard or surprised, you get a little startled and shaken."

"But why should that happen?"

"Well, there could be many reasons. What are you worried will happen when someone drops an assignment on you . . . (etc.)."

The idea is to get people to look at what's happening, what they're feeling, who's with them, and other similar details. Get them away from the amorphous floating feelings of helplessness. Good interviewers are not only eliciting details for their own information but also so the interviewees themselves can look at the data, too. The process of gathering information is in itself a helpful process, and that's why interviewing is such an important art to master, and one that takes a good deal of self control.

ANSWERING QUESTIONS WITH QUESTIONS

To prematurely jump in and offer feedback without giving time for both of you to grasp the specifics of the problem is sheer folly. Watch what happens when the bait is taken by the interviewer to give advice early in the game.

Mr. J. has been speaking for about fifteen minutes about his marital problems. During this time he has highlighted the fact that he is often busy at work and that this irritates his wife. Suddenly he stops and asks, "What do you think I can do to make the marriage work better?"

In response, Dr. W. quickly says, "Possibly you could spend more time with your wife. What do you think?"

"That's what everyone says. I wish it were that simple. What am I supposed to do? Give up my business? So we'll be together and have no money, then what? You're just like everyone else; you see only one side of it."

Another example which illustrates how easy it is to go astray when responding with a comment instead of a question is as follows:

Ms. B. had been speaking in a derogatory manner about her sister for about ten minutes. She then said, "And added to all I've told you she also just grabs my clothes and wears them without asking me. Isn't she a bitch?"

Dr. F., feeling the pressure of the question, responded almost without thinking, "It's true it seems that she isn't taking your feelings into consideration, but. . . ."

Quickly Ms. B. interjected—having heard almost exactly what she wanted to—"I knew you'd feel that way. I'm glad you do. I was pretty sure I should move out and leave her holding the lease, but now I'm positive!"

The problem in the above two interactions is similar. The listeners failed to question the question and return to a silent stance. They failed to return the focus to the person in distress.

When questioned about this, both therapists felt it would have been "rigid and cowardly" to reflect the question back to the counselee. They thought they would sound too much like a caricature of a nondirective therapist. One of them related a funny story that was going around about a "super nondirective therapist" who answered *everyone's* question with a reflection of that question . . . even a worker at the clinic who needed directions on his first day there:

"Excuse me doctor, can you tell me where the men's room is?"
"You say you want to know where the men's room is?"
"Yes, I'd like to know where it is."
"It sounds like you'd really like to know."

(In an annoyed voice) "Yes, I would like to know."

"It seems like you're annoyed that you don't know where the men's room is."

(Now in an angry voice) "Yes, I want to know where it is; are you going to tell me or not?"

"It seems you're angry at me because you don't know where the men's room is."

(Moving around the desk toward the therapist) "What me *angry?* Don't be silly. When I rip up your office now it's going to be an act of love!"

Now while it is true that one can be too nondirective and ask questions at inappropriate times, in reality these occasions are rare. A low-key, well-directed question will be appropriate far more often than not.

Also, when counselors give their reasons for *answering* a question rather than first *questioning* it, they usually show they don't understand the principle behind querying counselees' questions. A common feeling is that when someone asks a question, *not* to answer it is an evasion, a way to get the pressure off the interviewer. This is not so.

The reason an interviewee's question is responded to with a question is to make sure that the interviewee's question is fully understood. In addition, it indicates to the interviewee that he or she has the responsibility to work toward a personal solution to the problem.

Answering questions without exploring them first does two things. First, it supports infantile reactions in counselees by implicitly agreeing they can't come up with answers themselves. Secondly, it stops the communication without allowing the person to reflect on the question to see what it may mean from a number of angles. This latter point is very important, because the actual question may be very different from the way it looks on first blush. For instance:

"Doctor, are there many people like me who are depressed?" (This question seems to be one that requires a yes or no answer on the basis of the therapist's knowledge of the world's statistics on depression.)

"I'm not sure what you're asking."

"Well, I just want to know if there are more people like me."

"What prompts the question?"

"Well, I guess I've been thinking, I wonder if I'm normal, or I'm a useless freak?"

"Can you tell me a little more about these feelings you've been having about yourself?"

(Person begins relating fears of going crazy, thoughts about being alone, and feelings of hopelessness.)

Now, in the above illustration, the therapist would never have gotten to the subsequent material if the first question had been answered without being explored. Also, to answer what had seemed initially to be the question would have been to move in the wrong direction.

Sometimes it's not easy to answer a question with a question because the interviewee may resent it at first. However, having a questioning attitude is essential because it demonstrates that you're not the "magic answer machine" and it shows faith in the person's ability to solve his or her own problem with a little support. The following example illustrates this point:

"What do you think I should do?"

"Well, what have you come up with?"

"Nothing, that's why I'm asking you."

"I hear your question, but I'm sure you've given this problem some thought, and I'd like to hear what you've come up with—whatever it might be."

"Is this all I can expect? More questions?"

"What were your expectations?'

"That you would give me some answers. I could ask myself questions without you."

"Yes, you could, but there is some value if together we look at the questions you've been asking yourself. Sometimes speaking about them out loud is helpful. So, let's look at what you've been thinking and feeling about the problem. Now, what kinds of things have you been feeling about the problem you've just related?"

DEALING WITH UNSATISFACTORY RESPONSES

There are times when a question is asked but the answer received is insufficient in some fashion. Possibly it is incomplete, vague, or doesn't seem even to be directed at what was asked. When this occurs, it is sometimes helpful to take steps to clear up the situation so a better answer can be secured.

The first step is to mentally review how the question was phrased. Possibly it was a poor or inadequately developed question. The next step is to attempt to rephrase it and present it again. If this still doesn't seem to produce results, we have to make a judgment: Is the person so sensitive to this topic that it's difficult for him or her to answer it? (And should I drop further questioning for now?) Or should I press further, noting that the person seems to be having difficulty understanding or answering what's being asked?

Such a judgment is difficult to make. If the person seems hypersensitive, then possibly it would be best to bring the issue up later on, or even at another meeting. However, in most cases pressing on gently would at least bring this area a bit more out in the open. To do this, a simple statement, such as "I guess I'm not making myself clear because I still don't know where you stand (or how you feel about)____" should bring the person sufficiently out in the open on the issue.

TRANSITIONS BETWEEN TOPICS

Sometimes a confused or ambiguous response to a question stems from the fact the helper or interviewer has jumped from topic to topic without giving enough thought to making any connection between the different areas. While a relationship may exist in the mind of the helper, the person seeking assistance might not be in a position to see the connection and feel jolted by the change in focus.

Our awkwardness in changing topics may cause anxiety in the other person. A transitional technique is sometimes helpful in preventing such anxiety. This is especially so during the middle or near the end of the conversation.

In the beginning of the contact, we should try not to interrupt the person unless it is essential to do so. In most cases opening up and ventilating one's emotions is more important initially than organization or expansion of the information. Consequently, when the contact first begins, listening attentively is the most valuable "action" we can take.

After fifteen minutes to a half an hour has passed, though, enough clues should be out in the open for both people present to examine together. At this point, and *at the pace of the interviewee*, the interviewer can start to focus and expand on a number of areas.

Most of us don't have unlimited time to spend with a friend, employee, or family member, so wanting to cover a number of perspectives in working out a problem is quite natural. To do this efficiently and smoothly, making a definite transition can be helpful.

When enough material has been presented by the person to permit a clear understanding of the issues at hand, the following steps should be taken to move the process along: (1) interrupt, (2) clarify material gathered through feedback, and (3) change the topic to an allied area.

Let's say a friend of yours, Bill, is reporting how disgusted he is working as a truck driver. The point has come in the narrative where you think you have a good sense of the situation he's in now. The question which seems to logically follow is, "What else can he do other than stay in what he terms 'a dead-end position'?" How do you move on to this area without offending Bill who still seems deep in the story, but whom you must stop soon because you have an appointment in twenty minutes?

Here's how the three steps can be put into action: "Excuse me a minute Bill. Let me see if I have it straight. You say being a driver has turned out to be a really dead-end position. The only way you can make more money is to work longer hours and you're already putting in fifty-two hours a week. What's making it even more frustrating is you feel the work is getting too heavy for you, and you're tired of getting stuck with any old truck—often without a heater and sometimes with questionable brakes. Well, since all this stuff is getting to you, what do you think are the options open to you, other than continuing as a driver?"

When moving from topic to topic, it is important to give a good summary of what you've heard before moving on to another area. Sometimes you may not have gotten the exact impression the person is trying to relay. Thus, after giving the summarized feedback, it gives the narrator a chance to correct any misconceptions.

In the above illustration, Bill might have stepped in and said something to alter the impression you had. For instance, "Everything you said is on the mark, but believe me it's not the heavy work that bothers me so much. It's just that there seems to be no future if I stay where I am."

Once this correction takes place, the interviewer takes note of it and moves on to the next area. "Well, o.k. Given the fact there's no future Bill, what's open to you in terms of options to change the situation?"

Interviewing is an interpersonal process designed to secure information. Interviewing is not easy—just as active listening isn't possible without effort. Yet interviewing, like any purposeful communicative pursuit, can be productive and rewarding if a number of practical techniques are understood and if it is undertaken with high motivation.

Chapter 4

Tuning In to Others

Through active listening and the use of practical interviewing techniques we hope to gain a good deal of information about the people we deal with and the complaints they present. Yet the more we learn, the greater our realization is that understanding others is, at best, a very complex undertaking. To understand other people as best as possible, we must take special steps in an effort to meet them on their own ground.

Two steps we can take to increase our chances of understanding another are (1) trying to adopt the other person's internal frame of reference, and (2) being critical of the way we react to the complaints other people present.

ADOPTING THE OTHER'S FRAME OF REFERENCE

Whether we actually succeed in getting a good grasp of another's situation or not depends on a number of factors, but attempting to put yourself in the other person's position is a major first step in gaining a better understanding of those who come to us in distress.

If someone appears anxious about revealing a sensitive issue of a personal nature, we may take some steps to show we're in tune with the person and his current situation. We know if we were in that position, we'd want to take our time and not be rushed. With this in mind, special efforts can be made simply to allow the person to move ahead at a slow pace.

This may be the only thing that comes to mind. Still, even if it were the only way we could think of to reach out, it probably will make some type of positive impact.

No one can be *totally* empathetic. Thinking so is foolish, and attempting to be so will be futile. Moreover, most people, with the exception of the very demanding, don't expect total empathy. They see as encouraging any sign that the person they've come to is simply making the effort to reach out in their direction.

This seems to hold true in any type of interpersonal encounter. If you're telling a joke, you appreciate the friend who is smiling in anticipation of the conclusion as compared to old stoneface, an acquaintance who you know is not going to laugh no matter what.

In working toward getting a grasp of how the person feels in his/her current position, there are a number of simple steps we can take. Many of them we already take automatically. This is fine. The only drawback is that when we are not actively aware of these steps or techniques, we can't guarantee their presence each time. Similarly, their implementation and improvement is sometimes stunted since they're given little attention.

In trying to grasp another person's position, ask yourself a number of questions:

How would you feel about sharing the kind of problem the other person is describing? How do you think that person feels about sharing it?

What would you expect of someone to whom you were relating a personal difficulty? What do you think the other person expects of you?

How could someone put you at ease? How might you put this person at ease?

It's important to cue in on the nonverbal signs and the kinds of things being said. By adding these impressions to your answers to the above questions, you will be better able to appreciate the situation the other person is in. Unless this effort is made, you run the risk of seeing the other person in a vacuum and losing sight of the human context of the situation.

If, for example, a youngster is telling you why he failed an exam, he might do a number of things. One of the things he might do is omit certain details that make him look bad. He might even distort certain factors to make his failure look reasonable.

Seeing his statement in a vacuum rather than in a human context (*his* context) might cause us to react to the omissions and distortions. "Kenneth you say you didn't have enough time to study, the teacher wasn't fair, and there was material on the test which you hadn't been assigned. Who do you think you're kidding? You'd better get your act together, mister—and fast!"

How do you think this youth will react? Probably the same way you and I did—with resentment. We felt we weren't understood and saw our parents as tyrants. As we grew older we saw that they had our best interests in mind, but some of us came to believe that setting limits didn't have to take such a heartless form.

Furthermore, omitting things and providing minor distortions in portraying ourselves is something we all do. Suppose you were in a group setting and were asked to introduce yourself and say something about your background. Do you think you'd tell potentially harmful things about yourself? "I'm a college graduate, mother of four, my husband is ugly, and I stole apples from the fruitstand when I was eight years old." No way! You, like practically everyone else, would be trying to impress your new acquaintances with how great you are. It's natural. It's human. So to condemn it in others is ridiculous.

Putting yourself in the other person's position can lead you to deal with what they are telling you in a positive way. In the case of the youth who did poorly in his test, think of how he must be feeling. How did *you* feel when you didn't do well in school? Then your handling of him might be more like the following:

> "There seems to be a lot of reasons why you didn't do as well as you'd like. What can you do about it so you do better next time?"
>
> "Well, I'd like to give that teacher a piece of my mind."
>
> "I'm sure you would, but that wouldn't help. How could you alter your study habits so you're not caught off guard by a surprise test, or one that is more far-ranging than the lectures?"

In this interaction, the student is not being put on the defensive. Instead, he's being put at ease for a failure that can't be changed, and prepped for having to take full responsibility for his next performance. Being able to identify with him and his situation, and with others who come to us with a difficulty, should help us in opening up new constructive ways of handling the problem.

CRITICIZING OUR REACTIONS

Since our personality provides us with a special way of viewing the external world, we must be careful not to perceive things within too narrow a framework. If we are too narrow-minded, our biases may cause us to misinterpret information, or miss data on the one hand and exaggerate it on the other.

To correct for our biases, we must be our own devil's advocate. We must have the courage to critique our own decisions, immediately after they are formed. This will serve to relax the rigid channels we sometimes follow when taking in information and judging it.

One way to check our thinking is to take a position opposite to the one we've reached and try to support that opposite position reasonably and thoughtfully. While it probably won't cause us to change our overall impression, in many instances it might help us see some things in a slightly different light. At the very least, it will put us in a good position to liberalize our thinking and uncover our prejudices.

Our prejudices have not been reasoned into us. Therefore, they cannot be reasoned out. The only thing we can do about them is to attempt to be alert and try to uncover them at every turn. Then once we spot it, try to deal with it in an open fashion.

People can't help being prejudiced in some way. Our likes and dislikes have been programmed into us at the preverbal and preschool ages. Our tastes have been long in the making, and as we get older the sources and extent of them multiplies. I'm not referring to prejudice only in the narrow sense of racial prejudice. What I am talking about is the broad range of unconscious, usually unobtrusive, but unsupportable likes and dislikes we have.

Our likes and dislikes are not always bad in themselves. We all have our own preferences in clothing style, our own favorite pastimes, and so on. The problem with a prejudice for or against something occurs when it interferes with our intelligent assessment of someone or something. Such interference can extend to a point where we are making poor decisions which have an impact on our lives.

In trying to understand a person, elicit data, and work with him or her, prejudice can have a negative impact both in obvious and in subtle ways. It may be as simple as, "He reminds me of my cousin Steve, and boy do I *dislike* my cousin Steve." Or, it could be more subtle. "I met a woman named Carol today, and even before she spoke I knew I was going to like her."

Although the effects of negative bias have been widely publicized, the impact of positive prejudice has not received such attention. Yet positive bias can interfere as much when interviewing or counseling someone as can its negative counterpart. Good feelings toward someone *can* be a hinderance. That it's easier to work with someone who's likable is not a dispute. But the fact is that just as we miss important information when we become angry, we can also miss certain elements when we feel very favorably toward the other person.

Consequently, when working with someone we feel very positively toward, we still need to be a devil's advocate in regards to our reactions. For example, if a close friend, who is an easy-going pleasant person, tells us of a number of incidences in which her husband humiliated her, it is natural to side with her. No one likes to see a nice person taken advantage of by someone else. Still we still must say to ourselves, "Now that I feel she is being exploited and humiliated by her horrible husband, let me ask the question of myself, 'What if I'm all wrong and she is the culprit?' " While this question by itself may seem foolish, it may open the door to new information. It will prevent us from totally blaming the husband and aid us in examining more fully the participating role of the wife.

Asking the woman, "Why does he do it to you?" or "Why do you let him do it to you?" will probably lead to a nonproductive answer such as, "I don't know, I just don't know." By focusing on the part the apparently innocent woman plays, however, some light may be shed on how the interactions between husband and wife foster this behavior. By picturing the wife in an exaggerated role, in complete opposition to our feeling that her husband is a cad, questions which may prove more useful might come to mind. These useful questions will be ones that focus on the woman's *active* role in the problem.

Some of these questions might be as follows: Under what circumstances does he react hostilely? How do you react when he treats you this way? What prompts you to handle the situation in the way you do? How often does this happen? What's changed in your relationship? When did it change?

When we feel warmly toward someone, it's very hard for us to believe that it takes two to tango. However, problems usually arise *between* people and depend on the interaction between people, so it is the relationship that must be focused on, not the merits or faults of isolated "heroes" and "cads".

Anyone can side with a friend, but a helper can be even more valuable if she or he aids their friend to see what's happening more clearly. If a person can begin to see how his behavior is making the situation worse, or can view the twisted kind of advantage they maintain by maintaining the status quo, then the results can be most startling.

In the above situation, for example, we may find out the ways in which the wife encourages verbal battles. We may also uncover the "advantage"of her continuing with such a relationship: "We never seem to talk anymore—the only time I can get his attention is when we argue." This is not a healthy or positive reason for arguing and allowing oneself to be humiliated. Yet a need for attention in a deteriorating and lonely marriage may be the impetus behind this woman's behavior. Such situations are sad, especially since her behavior does not permit this woman to change or grow.

A DISTORTED VIEW OF THE HELPER

Up to this point we have spoken about the distorted view we may have of a person coming in and asking for help. But distorted views can exist on both sides. We must be aware that a friend, colleague, or family member who asks for help may have a distorted perception of us.

Their misperceptions of us can take a number of forms, and trying to anticipate what they will be is a frustrating waste of time. The important thing is to be alert to their possible presence so that we can better respond to the person's predicament.

Quite often a person will emphasize a particular view of you because of the problem they're experiencing. If the person is troubled by finances, for example, you as the helper may be cast as a financially well-off individual, even though you're in the same league as far as expenses and resources go. If the person is quite depressed, you may be seen as happy-go-lucky and secure. If they are having difficulty in personal relations, they will distort your ability to interact with others. If it's a younger person, you may be told you never had these problems. Or the very reason they say they're talking to you ("You have such a happy marriage") will often turn out to be the reason they believe you can't help them ("What would you know about marriage problems?").

The fact that a person seeking your help alternately praises you or condemns you is a function of how he or she feels, not a function of who or what you really are. In therapy, such projections on the part of clients are dealt with very carefully. In counseling family and friends it's best to take the inflated compliments and deflating put-downs with a block, not just a grain, of salt.

Nor should one fall into the trap of inwardly accepting such misperceptions of oneself. You might try to live up to them by making believe you're someone you aren't, or waste energy maintaining a role someone else seems to appreciate.

The way to handle the person's distortions is either to ignore them or to gently try to correct them. Realize what they are, don't get confused or misled by them, and don't waste time arguing. It won't help them and it may get you upset. An even-tempered, supportive listener who appreciates how easy it is for someone to distort when under stress can accomplish much.

DEFENSIVE STYLES

People have different ways of behaving under stress, different "defensive styles." While these behaviors have a common cause, namely our feelings of anxiety or conflict, we manifest

our feelings in different ways. Some of us get nervous and
defensive, some put up a front that "all is well"; others of us
wish we could just fall apart and let someone else handle it.
Recognizing the basic way a person is reacting to stress—
recognizing his or her defensive style—is a great advantage in
helping that person deal with whatever is at issue.

There are many ways people defend themselves. However in
the following sections we shall look at the five which seem most
predominant. They are false courage or denial, childlike behavior, hostility, depression, and evasion. We may see these styles
in combination with each other or perhaps only in a minor way,
but knowing about them can be quite valuable. Recognizing
them, they can give us an insight into how the person we're
dealing with acts when in trouble and can help us respond in the
most appropriate way.

FALSE COURAGE OR DENIAL

False courage is one of the most common styles of dealing
with stress. This "macho," "stiff-upper-lip" approach is frequently used by people uncomfortable with facing any personal
feelings of inadequacy.

"Keeping a stiff upper lip" is often defended in western society. In England and her stepchild America, the belief is that we
should prevent expressions of emotion and fight dependency at
all cost. We also mistakenly equate being unemotional and
being strong and in control.

The kernel of truth in this myth is that self-control in a crisis *is*
better than falling apart. If someone gets a sleeve caught in a
moving conveyor belt, obviously it's better to keep your cool
and run to shut off the machine than to throw your tools up in
the air and just stand there and yell.

However, while self-control is essential for effective action, it
does not preclude admitting one's predicament or temporarily
leaning on someone. But the person using false courage does

not admit this. Instead, he finds facing a problem so repug-
nant that he consciously or unconsciously suppresses the severity of the problem. Frequently such an individual will even
go a step further and act in a way directly opposed to the
weakness they feel (in mental health jargon, this is referred
to as "reaction formation").

The incongruities which result are usually obvious to everyone but the person involved. A student failing his senior year in
high school may be filling out applications for Harvard and
Yale. An aerospace engineer slated to lose her job may be
spending money like she's getting a promotion next week. A
man who's having problems in his marriage may be describing it
in glowing terms fashion to his closest friends.

Due to the massive denial and great fear of appearing weak,
this type of person is very difficult to deal with effectively. In
most cases, the best thing one can do is provide general support
and point out some of the incongruities in as nonthreatening a
way as possible. Confrontation accomplishes little, if anything,
with this kind of individual.

With the failing student who is applying to Harvard, there
would be little point in criticizing his choice or removing his
fantasy. Instead, something might be achieved by discussing
with him how he plans to raise his failing grades so he doesn't
miss fall enrollment. In addition, when he gives this information and it is explored as much as he permits, then some
attention can be given to how he could be hedging his bets
by applying to other colleges, a practice employed by all
good students.

What we are trying to do with this type of person is to provide
support for them and show faith in their problem-solving abilities. Expressing agreement with their exaggerated behavior
(applying to Harvard) is not necessary. You may be the only
person who doesn't laugh at him, so the student in this illustration might want you to agree with him. To agree that he's
acting sensibly would be deceptive. However you can share his
feelings and support his efforts without putting him down:

"You seem O.K. Not like the others. You don't think I'm silly applying to Harvard do you?"

"What do you think about your applying to Harvard?"

"Well, I really want to do it, but everybody thinks I'm stupid. I guess that's why I want to know what you think."

"Well, I'm more interested in the whole range of schools you've applied to rather than just Harvard."

"But I'm really excited about Harvard, but no one else seems to back me up."

"Why do they feel that way? . . ."

A person showing false courage is avoiding a problem, and you cannot force them to face it. Pushing them is not helping them. But, as described in chapter 2, the helper can be alert to verbal and nonverbal cues and reflect them back to the individual to see if this will open up avenues for discovery and problem-solving. Take, for example, the case of the man heartily describing his marriage, while suppressing the difficulties in it:

"Oh, Alice couldn't be better! She's a great gal. Starting her own business, too!"

"Oh, that sounds exciting."

"Yeah, I'm all for it. Gets her out of the house, you know. It's something she's always wanted. I'm all for it."

"You look a little down in the mouth when you say that, though . . ."

Depending upon his response to your remark, his feelings on the matter can then be explored as far as he permits.

CHILDLIKE BEHAVIOR

Childlike behavior is another defensive style commonly displayed by people under stress. This kind of person seems immobilized by problems. In a pleading voice they ask, "What am I going to do?" Anxiety, conflict, and frustration push them to regress to a temporary, dependent role. They want to be parented, hugged, and led around—though often they seem to resist and fight your directive efforts if you try to be mother or father to them.

This kind of style can be quite annoying. The temptation for some of us is to say, "Snap out of it!" Telling this type of individual to shape up or ship out usually accomplishes little. At most, they may be temporarily pushed to action, but this activity will soon cease.

One of the most effective ways of handling this type of individual is to behave toward them in a manner which indicates your faith in the person's ability to deal with the situation competently. Your behavior should seem to say, "You're independent and have resources, you can handle it."

Now there is a big difference between *saying* this to a person and *modeling* the message through your behavior. In saying the words, the result is often an ineffective pep talk that will leave you, the helper, quite frustrated. Modeling the message is done through interacting with the person in a way which demonstrates your belief in his ability to get himself and the situation together. Demonstrate your faith not by giving advice, but by being quiet and nondirective and asking them what they feel and think they should do.

"I just don't know what to do. What should I do? What would you do in my place?"

"Well, what do you think you should do?"

"I don't know. What do you think?"

"Well, there must be something you would *like* to do."

"There are things I know I should do, but I can't."

"What do you think you should do then?"

"I should forget the marriage and divorce him."

"What makes you think you should do that?"

"Well, it seems like my only choice, so I have to do it."

"You could do it, but think out loud about the other options you might have."

"Do you think there are other options? What do you think they would be?"

"You're in the situation and know yourself and your husband better than I. I'd be interested in hearing you bring up some of the alternatives open to you, other than breaking up with him."

In the above conversation, the interviewer is trying to keep the focus and problem-solving responsibility on the dependent person. As can be seen, it's often not easy. However, jumping in and rescuing this type of person accomplishes little in the long run, even though it might seem easy to do at the time.

Also illustrated in the above vignette is that people often put off making a decision because they feel the only really effective way of solving the problem is to change the situation dramatically (e.g., getting a divorce), and this scares them. The dependent type must be helped to criticize the style of thinking which leads to these conclusions. In this case, the woman has asked support for her belief that she should divorce her husband, that this is the only alternative. It may be. However, final decisions like that should be made only after other options have at least been entertained.

HOSTILITY AND DEPRESSION

Hostility also rears its head when certain kinds of individuals are under stress and seeking help. After dropping hints about their present problems, they show hostility or at least suspicion when someone goes to intervene.

Like the bravado of those who display false courage, this type of individual is worried about being vulnerable. The gnawing fear is, "If they see I'm not doing so well, what will they think of me? And how will they then treat (exploit) me?"

Due to this fear, they strike out first through hostility. Their thinking is, "Get them first, since they will take advantage of me if they have a chance." The result is that people shy away from them, which supports their original fear that people are not *really* interested in them. These are the kinds of people we're constantly avoiding or making the statement to them, "Now, don't be like that. I'm only trying to help."

Hostility may also take the form of a displaced anger. While they are with the cause of their difficulty they are quiet. Then they come into contact with someone who is nice to them and bang! the anger gets redirected from the original target onto them.

No one enjoys taking a verbal thrashing from a friend, but if you realize where the anger is really directed, you can point it out. Also, by recognizing that the person's hostility is due to anxiety, it's a bit easier not to feel so personally affected by his comments.

A fourth way of reacting to problems is depression. This reaction is familiar to all of us. In fact, depression is so common that it will be given separate treatment in Chapter 7. For now though, it will be enough to emphasize that dealing with the depressive style of handling problems requires patience and detachment on the part of the helper.

Depressive persons can drag you down with them if you aren't alert to this basic principle: *You can't help a depressed person over a period of time if you join in their sadness, or if you expect them to improve too quickly.*

This is more easily said than done. In our efforts to be empathetic, getting caught up with the person's helplessness and hopelessness is quite easy. Likewise, in our action-oriented society, trying to get a lethargic, emotionally depressed person to start moving again is a natural goal.

However, motivating a depressed individual is not easy. Hope must be held out for them. Yet improvement must be seen in terms of slow progress over time, and both helper and counselee must have patience with a seeming lack of forward movement.

EVASION

The final style of reacting to stress is evasion. Evasion is a
blocking out of information from our conscious thoughts, and it
is a common manner of handling difficult situations. We frequently employ evasion when we avoid potentially disturbing
situations and when we try to ignore existing problems in our
lives.

For instance, we occasionally try to avoid hearing bad news.
We shut off the TV as they are about to report on starvation in
India. We quickly turn the page of the paper rather than read a
story on a rape incident. We do this because such news disturbs
us. For any number of reasons, we would rather avoid these
stories. For us, for the moment, these problems don't exist.
We're determined to put them out of our mind.

Evasiveness can also take the form of avoiding an existing
personal problem, rather than dealing directly with it. When
people bring the problem up, some of us give brief, simplified
answers and change the subject. Other people will joke about it
rather than deal with an uncomfortable issue. Still others just
ignore what is being said.

Various messages are being sent by us and other people when
we do this. One of them is, "Leave me alone. It's too overwhelming at this point. Let someone else take the responsibility
for handling it, because I surely am not ready to do it."

When we deal with massive blocking on the part of patients
who are extremely disturbed, we move very slowly at opening
up these areas. However, in dealing with someone who is
basically healthy and just seems to desire to avoid an issue, it
can be handled more actively.

One way this can be done is by pointing to the fact that the
person is avoiding a topic and indicating that you appreciate
that the topic must be upsetting to them. If someone says, "I
don't want to talk about it!", you can at least indicate, "Well you

must be pretty upset if you don't want to talk about it." If this, too, meets with a refusal to discuss it, then it might be best to say one additional thing. "Well, if you don't want to talk about it now, it's O.K. But you'll have to talk about it with someone sometime if it's ever going to get resolved."

Some people think it's best not to pursue an issue if someone is evasive or openly refuses to talk about it. This isn't necessarily the best route. When someone refuses to discuss a matter, remaining silent is tantamount to agreeing that the subject must indeed be so unapproachable that he is right in not wanting to talk about it, or, worse yet, in not wanting to face it.

Reinforcing such positions is incorrect. This doesn't mean we should push, push, push. As indicated above, we should not agree with their premise, but instead give them the feeling it's O.K. if they want to *postpone* talking about it. This way, we respect their right to silence, while disagreeing with their fear of facing the supposedly terrible issue.

The major defensive styles covered here are not the only ones people use when dealing with stress, and they should not be seen as mutually exclusive. The hostile person, for example, may also exhibit childish behavior.

In discussing these defenses, the goal is not to point out pathological styles but merely to indicate that people respond in different ways when they are boxed in by their own frustrations or environment. To understand these styles, even on a very elementary level, is to better appreciate the person and the problem. In recognizing how a person is acting, we can better intervene with them as well. We will be less likely to be put off when someone is hostile because he or she is upset. The chances are less that we'll join in with an evasive person in supporting their evasions. We will be better able to maintain a helpful stance towards the depressed person, rather than getting dragged down or frustrated by him. Learning to recognize defensive styles is not so we can label people, it is so we can better understand them.

The aim of this entire chapter has been to foster greater rapport with the person seeking help through an appreciation of how it is to be in the other person's shoes and why a person comes across as he does. This appreciation is essential. The goal is to see how a person comes across in terms of how they perceive their situation, rather than in terms of ourselves. Otherwise, we might get bogged down in worrying why a person is treating us with hostility, or be put off by a fear of never grasping what the person is going through. Tuning in to others and understanding their behavior greatly increases our ability to help.

Chapter 5

The Goals of Counseling

The preceding chapters have examined three particular aspects of counseling: how to listen, how to question, and how to try to understand the other's situation. You hopefully have a better idea now of how to hear another person out, of how to respond with appropriate questions, of how to interpret the other's words and behavior. Let us now back off a bit to gain some perspective on the ends to which our counseling skills are directed. What are the goals of counseling? What object do we keep in mind as we listen, question, and interpret?

Counseling can be many things and have many purposes. It can be conducted in accordance with any number of theories. However, there is one thing that counseling is not, and that is intensive psychotherapy.

The distinction between counseling and therapy is an important one. Therapy's aim is personality change. It is an in-depth process requiring specific and extensive education and expertise. Therapy can take considerable time, since it is utilized with problems that can be quite severe.

To put everyone who experiences some degree of anxiety, depression, or stress in therapy would be ridiculous. For these people, for the people who come to us for help with some situational or emotional difficulty, counseling, not therapy, is the more appropriate technique. I am in agreement with Dr. Leona Tyler, who defines counseling as "a helping process the aim of which is not to change the person but to enable him to utilize the resources he now has for coping with life. The outcome we would then expect from counseling is that the client *do* something, take some constructive action on his own behalf." (Leona E. Tyler, *The Work of the Counselor* New York: Appleton-Century-Crofts, 1961, p. 12).

The object then is not to change the person, give advice, or solve a problem. Instead the goal is to open up the means for the person to do his own problem-solving with resources he or she already has. Counseling is thus a guided process of explortion and discovery. The emphasis is on examining a situation, identifying resources, and clarifying reasonable alternatives and goals. The person will do his own decision-making and problem solving. The counselor simply helps him or her uncover the means to do so.

Counselors help the person do his own problem-solving through (1) reflecting the person's emotions, (2) focusing on the person's assets as well as limitations, (3) helping the person clarify the issues and behaviors involved, and (4) helping the person identify and evaluate alternatives.

EXPLORING FEELINGS

One of the things counselors are best known for is the effort they take to make counselees aware of the counselee's own feelings about the issues and people they discuss. This is an important undertaking because, where emotions are strong, they will surely affect the person's actions and opinions.

Anger, disgust, elation, love, hate, warmth, fear, annoyance—these feelings can alter a perception in such a way that the person becomes mired in distortion. There's nothing intrinsically wrong with emotions. But when they are so exaggerated that they prevent someone from taking personal control, or when a person is so unaware of their presence that their influence on the situation is ignored, then they inhibit the person's problem-solving ability and are an unwanted interference.

So reflecting and exploring emotions is an important goal in counseling. It permits the person to open up, to identify and evaluate the feelings he has. The fascinating thing about reflecting a person's emotions is the complexity it unearths in the way people feel about things. While most of us single out one emotion to describe our reaction to an event, we actually feel an array of them.

For instance, many people say how angry they are, but smile as they report the incident. Others say they feel confident about something, but their eyes say otherwise. These things have to be pointed out to the person. If they aren't, the ambivalence they feel will be missed.

"Bill, you say you're angry, but you're smiling as you say it."

"Well, she does upset me, but I do get a kick out of her spunk. I've never gone out with someone who has told me to go to hell quite the way she has."

"So, you're angry about . . .?"

"Well, I'm angry that she didn't go along with my plan to stay home and just watch TV. I was bushed and was low on cash. She should have had more consideration and I thought what a bitch she was."

"But the spunk sort of surprised you in a pleasant way."

"Yeh, since I'm such a big deal at college, most of the girls I've been with have gone along with what I wanted. She didn't and it was a nice change, though I don't know whether I could take a steady diet of someone like her."

"What do you mean?"

By focusing in on both the emotions Bill held toward his friend's actions, the whole topic of his attitudes and fears about women is opened up. Feelings are important. They are tied to beliefs and to personal and interpersonal concerns. They are worth getting out in the open.

Feelings also need to be defined. More and more, we are finding that getting people to elaborate on the feelings they claim is extremely useful. They get to see in greater detail the many aspects and ramifications of their reported emotions.

> "I'm quite annoyed over the way my boss handled the situation. There I am in front of several of the people who work for me and he reads me the riot act."
>
> "You're annoyed?"
>
> "Yeh, he has got to be kidding. (*Voice is getting louder; face is starting to tighten up.*) What are they going to think of me now? Who does he think he is anyway?"
>
> "You say you're annoyed, but you seem more angry than merely annoyed."
>
> "I guess I am. I really looked bad."
>
> "It must make you angry looking so bad in front of your subordinates."
>
> "You're not kidding! What are they going to think of me?"
>
> "After that episode, you sound a bit concerned about the way your people are going to see you."
>
> "I am concerned, suppose they start feeling, 'Well, he's a real loser; look how the boss treats him.' It bothers me." (*Starting to sound quite down about the situation.*)
>
> "It really does bother you, doesn't it?"
>
> "It really does."
>
> "This thing seems to have you really down."
>
> "Boy, it does. I get worried when someone does something like that to me."
>
> "What worries you about that kind of treatment? You sound like it's happened to you before."

In the above illustration, the depth of the emotions was explored. What was described at first as annoying was actually very upsetting. What initially appeared to be concern, turned into worry which was leading to depression. The emotions turned out to be more serious than was initially reported. If the initial reports were accepted and not questioned, we would never have understood how this person really felt or the true scope of the underlying problem.

In reflecting the person's emotions, we use *their* words, or synonyms for them, to get them to talk further about how they feel. We also key in on their nonverbal signs and what they indicate about the person's feelings (see chapter 2). Then together with the person, we can examine those feelings.

One positive result of reflecting a person's feelings, aside from getting an idea of the actual feelings involved and the scope of the problem, is the catharsis experienced by the person seeking help.

Such emotional release can be very beneficial. "Pressure cooker" is a label which applies to many of us today. In our mobile society, people complain of having few friends to share their secrets with, too much stress to bear, and few ways to naturally let out their frustrations and pent-up emotions.

When people are able to get in touch with their feelings, one of the benefits is that they get a chance to let off steam. The result can be amazingly therapeutic. They start off a conversation feeling tense and jittery. We might think we accomplished little with them. Yet they leave us noticeably more relaxed and thankful for our help.

Comments like the following are not unusual:

"I feel so much better. Thanks for your help."

"Gee, that's a load off my chest. I appreciate your listening. You always were a good friend."

"I just needed someone to hear me out. It seems everyone is full of advice. They all have the answers, but they don't know how hard it is. I come over here and you sit there and are patient with me. I don't know what I'd do without you at times like these."

As people unload their troubles, the burden becomes lighter. They get a chance to look at what's going on and how they feel about it. In addition, they are able eventually to achieve some

objectivity toward the issues when they are out in the open.
This objectivity would not have been possible before, given the
tension they were under.

A potential hazard of reflecting a person's emotions is that it
can lead to a dead end. When this happens, breaking the circle
is easy—and essential.

> "It seems you feel down."
> "Yes, I really feel blue."
> "Boy, you do seem blue."
> "Yes. I am depressed."
> "You certainly seem depressed."

This kind of encounter is not getting anywhere. The person
has already expressed that he/she is not feeling up to par. The
counselor has reflected the feeling a number of times. If this
keeps up it would be natural for the client to say, "Well, we've
established that I'm depressed, blue, and down; now what?"

Without belittling the reflection process, which is essential to
get the client to open up and recognize the counselor's empathy
for the feelings involved, reflection cannot be used alone. As
was indicated in chapter 3, once an emotion is expressed in full,
more details are necessary. Namely, *when* did the person become depressed (or more depressed than normal)? Under *what
circumstances* did they become depressed? *With whom* do they
react this way? And, if necessary, *when* has this emotion occurred *in the past*. (This is done to elucidate a pattern of situations which produce the reaction. It is not conducted as a
psychoanalytic safari into the hidden past.)

Reflection of emotions is an essential aim of counseling. It
helps counselees get in touch with their real feelings, and it
helps counselors better understand other people and their problems. It is a way for us to show them we have a good idea of
what they are going through, how they are feeling, what they
are experiencing. It is very important not to slight the exploring
of feelings. Only after the process of reflection seems to be

going no further do we try to move to questions regarding circumstances. (Pacing of the conversation is discussed further in chapter 7.)

FOCUSING ON ASSETS

Counseling should be a balanced, positive undertaking. It must concern itself not only with a person's limitations, but it must also uncover and emphasize a person's assets. When it doesn't, progress becomes elusive.

Too often the processes of counseling and psychotherapy become an excursion into the lands of pathology and illness. Some helpers assume the role of healer and accept at face value the limitations people present in their narrative. They knowingly or unknowingly take the position, "This person is all messed up. I have to help them see what they are doing wrong, how inadequate their approaches are."

One goal of counseling is to elucidate the inappropriate or fruitless patterns of dealing with a situation. But to do so at the expense of opening up and emphasizing the resources a person has to solve the dilemma is a major mistake.

Counseling should not encourage infantile behavior in the client. If the person walks away feeling, "Yes, it's true; I'm really messed up!" then the session has been a failure. As much attention needs to be given to positive abilities as is paid to problematic liabilities. In the reflection process we reflect positive feelings ("You seem really happy about this") as much as we do negative ones. The same should be done in uncovering assets and limitations.

Frequently a person's difficulty is simply the "other side of the coin" of a similar positive trait.

For instance, a person who takes criticism too personally may run into problems. People may not want to be around him because they have a fear of offending him. However, in trying to get the person to see this pattern, we would not want to ignore the positive value of this person's sensitivity.

Many of us are not sensitive enough. This individual may possess a fine ability to be attuned to other people and the world at large. His interpretation of how people view him may be colored by an insecure perception of self. However in other instances, where a personal opinion is not involved, such distortions may not be present. So in discriminating when sensitivity is a problem, efforts must be made to also note when it is a help.

This is not accomplished by giving the person a pep talk or by mouthing general remarks that have nothing to do with the situation in question.

Comments like, "Look, you're O.K. Just don't think about the problem" are too general and ignore the troubles the person is experiencing. When comments are directed to what is going on and are related to both the person's assets and liabilities, they can be quite helpful.

"What they say about me is upsetting. I guess I'm just too sensitive. I care too much. I guess that's my problem. If I didn't worry about other people's perceptions of me, I'd be in a better place emotionally right now."

"But you do care."

"Yes, I do. I want to come across effectively. I want people to like me. I don't want to be seen as a terrible person."

"Well then, why wouldn't you want to continue to be the type of person who cares about other people's feelings and opinions?"

"Because it hurts too much."

"Does it hurt all of the time, or just when you feel they're saying negative things about you?"

"Oh, it's just when I feel they're putting me down."

"Do people ever give you feedback that they like it when you're sensitive to their needs and feelings?"

"Yes. In fact, people say I'm so considerate of them. They feel I'm tactful. I don't just open my mouth, say what I damn well please and hurt them like Maryann. She's someone who lives in the neighborhood. She never seems to have anything nice to say. Nor does she ever know when to keep quiet."

"So your being sensitive to others causes you problems only when the comments are directed to you, or you feel they are?"

"Yes. That's right."

"So, what we need to look at is not your ability to be sensitive to your environment, but when this gets you into trouble in terms of feeling put down by others?"

"Yes. That's right. If I could just figure out why little statements get to me."

"Well, when was the last time someone said something to you that hurt?"

(Person goes on to describe incident and both she and the counselor look at it together for clues.)

In the above illustration, there's an effort to discriminate, an effort to show that the person's sensitivity isn't generally bad, but only selectively a problem. In certain instances it is even a plus. Then an illustration is requested. This is done so the person can begin to see the problem not as something mysterious, but something which can be brought into more distinct focus.

After the illustration is presented, then further resource utilization will take place. The person will be asked to problem-solve with the counselor. They will look at the circumstances together to see what happened, how he/she felt, and how the bad feelings which resulted might have been avoided or lessened. By doing this, people get the message that they are still able to act and to take charge of their own lives. They are also better able to accept that a seemingly confused and problematic situation can be clarified and that their present difficulties are only temporary.

CLARIFYING ISSUES

A key aim of counseling is to enable counselees to take constructive action on their own behalf. But their ability to do so

depends upon uncovering their own problem-solving skills.
When people come to us for help, it is often because their
problem-solving abilities seem paralyzed. The more they act,
the more they see themselves being pulled down in interpersonal quicksand.

> "I don't know what to say to her anymore."
> "What do you mean?"
> "Well, it seems the more I try to discuss her late hours and
> her running around, the more she resents it. In the past we
> used to talk about things. She listened to me. Now, when I
> tell her what I think, she gets angry and storms out. I just
> don't know what to do. If I can't discuss things with her,
> what chance do I have of making any kind of impact. I feel
> so helpless."

When people come to us, futility and frustration often darken
their outlook and are reflected in their downtrodden carriage
and sad facial expression. There seems to be no way out. If
there are any alternatives, either they don't see them, or they
don't like them. The message they give us is that unless something drastic happens, the situation cannot be solved—at least
not by them.

Due to the apparent hopelessness of it all, they seem to want
to hear two different things: "Yes, you're right, the situation is
hopeless" and "This is going to be easy because I know the
magical solution to the problem." While many people don't
really believe either message, they feel that both might somehow be true because they cannot see any alternatives.

Counselors must handle this kind of despondency with care.
If we start to feel the hopelessness of the person, we may
become despondent too. We may also rush around mentally in
an effort to come up with a neat new idea to solve the troubles at
hand. Neither action is helpful or rewarding.

What is usually helpful is to re-examine what the person is
doing to alleviate the problem. Feeling caught in a frustrating,

seemingly hopeless muddle can be the result of the person's not recognizing what he is or is not doing in certain circumstances. Re-examining the person's behavior can help clarify the issues and open up alternatives and possible solutions to the difficulty.

"You say you've discussed the situation with your daughter. It seems to make it worse and that in the past this wasn't the case."

"Yes, that's right."

"Do you perceive any change in the way you discuss things with your daughter over the past year?"

"I'm not sure what you mean?"

"Well has your style changed in how you broach topics with her?"

"No. Not that I'm aware of. It's more her changing toward me. In the past she listened to me. Followed my instructions. Now she doesn't."

"So, in the past she would hear you out calmly; then take your advice?"

"Calmly? Are you kidding?"

"Ah. She reacted in the past as she reacts now?"

"Yes. She has always been a hot head. Only then I could convince her."

"You mean she would wind up agreeing with you all of the time?"

"No. She rarely felt I was right all of the time. It's just that she was more respectful. I had control over her. She listened to me."

"So, what has changed then is her going along with you?"

"Yes, it seems she doesn't listen anymore."

"And by 'doesn't listen' you mean she hears what you have to say, doesn't agree, and acts according to how she feels concerning the matter."

"That's right."

"Well, I'm not clear then about your feelings that she doesn't hear you out. That she doesn't seem to be open to discussing things with you as in the past."

"If she would sit down and talk things over, she'd see I'm right. You have to be there. I just start telling her and she gets up and storms out. How would you feel?"

"How do you feel when she does that?"

"I get so angry I could smash her. I just don't know what to do."

"How does she feel during these interactions?"

"Who knows?"

"You said that in a voice as if you meant 'who cares.'"

"She gets me so angry. Wouldn't you get angry if your child wouldn't hear you out?"

"It seems, though, that you do care. What gets you angry doesn't appear to be the fact that she storms out as much as that she doesn't follow your advice anymore."

"All of it gets me angry, but I wish she'd listen to me . . . take my advice. She's going to get herself into a lot of trouble."

"If you could get her to hear you out, you might have a better chance to win her over. However, her staying to listen to you and her taking your advice are two different things, aren't they?"

"Well, I doubt if she'll listen to anything I have to say. She doesn't give me a chance."

"Does she feel you give her a chance?"

"It's funny that you say that. She's always said that I didn't take her feelings into account. But I've always had her best interests at heart. She's still a child. I am her mother."

"Yes, you are. She is nineteen though. In the past when you disagreed, you felt better because in the end she capitulated and followed your directives. Now your arguments seem to end in her doing what she wants and her being angry at you. You also end up being angry and frustrated with her."

"So, we're back to square one. I'm caught."

"Both of you are caught if you try to impose your will on her or if you angrily argue instead of discussing the alternatives."

"So, you think I should pamper her? You think I should let her do what she damn well pleases without objecting if I don't agree?"

"Is that what I said?"

"That's what I heard. You want me to *discuss* things with her. She'd never hear me out. You know she has a temper. It's not all *my* fault."

"Well, it's no wonder that you would not want to discuss things if you felt that was the same as agreeing with her, pampering her, and letting her do what she pleases. You may also be right that it will be hard to convince her that you just want to be heard out. She may react in an angry way in the beginning, thinking you're just trying to get her to do your bidding through another means. And, by the way, you might be determined to do just that."

"What do you mean?"

"Well, you have strong opinions on right and wrong. Discussion isn't real if you're not going to consider the possibility that you may be wrong. Also, discussion usually has as a ground rule that the other person has the right to decide that you're wrong and they're right. Are you willing to play by that ground rule?"

"I know she's not a child, but. . . ."

"You see, when you first came in, you complained that she didn't listen to you. That she wouldn't even discuss her going out late with you. This may not be the case. She may be willing to at least discuss things with you. As an adult."

"You mean it's my fault that she's this way?"

"No, I mean if you still want to discuss things with her, it still may be possible to do that. She may listen to you. She may be worried in the beginning that you're just trying a new tactic to win her over. So, at first she may be angry and be fearful that in the end you will win out and she'll be treated like a child again. But, if you want to at least get your views heard without arguing, there's reason to believe you still can do it."

"But there's no guarantee she'll listen."

"Is there any guarantee she's listening now?"

"No, that's just it. She's not listening; it's like she hates me."

"Hates you, or hates arguing and being dictated to?"

This fairly lengthy narrative points out a number of counseling principles. First, it demonstrates one way of focusing on a person's ability to recognize and change styles of interaction. This is done by uncovering and identifying several separate issues:

1. The daughter is no longer a child, but a young adult with a mind of her own.

2. Arguing and discussion are two different things.

3. What the mother sees as a hopeless situation is not definitely so. The frustration is arising from her unwillingness to try relating to her daughter in a different way. (This was brought out without going into, in any depth, her possible fears of losing control over her daughter, who is now entering adulthood.)

4. The mother sees having an open discussion with her daughter as being tantamount to pampering her child and letting her run wild.

5. Her daughter's love of her and her daughter's willingness to go along 100 percent while being treated as an ignorant, ill-behaved child are two different things. (The mother has probably long equated obedience with love.)

There's more in the interaction, but for our purposes now, the five points above are sufficient. The main emphasis has been to recognize and identify issues and behaviors. People are prevented from using their problem-solving talents when situations become confused. The confusion leads to feelings of frustration and hopelessness. Tempers rise or emotions fall, and the situation seems to be an irretrievable mess.

However, by not getting mixed up in the emotions of the

situation, we can calmly point out areas of confusion, emotion, vagueness, and strength. It's quite easy to get baited into reacting emotionally to the person having the problem. But we must be careful to stay on our toes and remain calm. If we get upset or frustrated, we will only compound the problem. To point out some of the issues to the person in a calm, straightforward fashion, while exploring the feelings the person has about the issues being covered, is our main objective in this case.

OPENING UP ALTERNATIVES

Once some of the relevant issues and behaviors have been identified and the problem no longer seems such a muddle, it will be easier for the counselee to see and explore alternative behaviors and solutions. This is where real problem solving comes in.

Problem solving centers on opening up alternatives which the counselee can accept as real for them. We, as counselors, are in the option business, not the brainwashing business, no matter how right we believe we are. Our purpose is not to solve a problem per se, but rather to introduce new perspectives and new avenues of approach, while accepting and supporting the other person's right to choose his or her own mode of action.

The following interaction explores a problem, clarifies some issues, and leads to the opening up of ways of dealing with the situation.

. . . "Well, tell me about your daughter's school problems before the suspension."

"She's never been a good student."

"What do you mean?"

"Well, she always just got by. We've been in for parent conferences again and again. My husband won't even go in anymore."

"How do you feel about that?"

"Well, I guess I can understand his being fed up with it all."

"But how do you feel all in all?"

"Well, to be honest, I'm tired, too. I hate to be the one who's always being called in because Jill isn't measuring up or is smoking in the back of the class. Can't they do anything?"

"So the problem isn't a new one?"

"Not by a long shot. Jill has been a pain in the neck for years as far as school goes."

"And it sounds like you feel you've been bearing the brunt of it, and are a bit angry at the school and your husband for not doing their share."

"Not exactly angry. I guess they've done their part."

"Whether they have or not is another story. You've been dealing with this problem for some time, though, and you sound a bit frustrated and angry, which would be natural under the circumstances."

"Well, I hate to admit it, but I guess I am. It gets to me."

"So how did you feel when you were told about the suspension?"

"As I said, I was upset. I could have brained her and the principal as well."

"How did you handle Jill when she came home?"

"I smashed her and sent her to her room. She's lucky I didn't kill her. I was livid."

"Did you say anything to her?"

"I just yelled. I probably told her the same things I usually say. That she's a problem. I get no peace. And that she's ruining her life. And if she wants to do that, it's o.k. with me."

"How did she react?"

"She started yelling at me that no one understood. She actually told me it was my fault and that the principal was a tight ass and didn't understand, either."

"What did you have to do regarding the school?"

"Well, I called the principal. I was angry, but I kept cool because I didn't want them to throw Jill out. She only has six months to graduation. She has to go back next week when her suspension is up. I've lectured her until I'm blue in the face. I don't know what else to do."

"What has the school's reaction been?"

"Well, the teacher says she's unruly and he just can't handle her, but will give it one more try. The principal says she has one more opportunity to prove herself."

"So you feel under the gun with regards to her returning."

"I sure do. My husband says he doesn't give a damn. They sound serious at school. And Jill, if you can believe it, says she's going to try hard."

"You have doubts?"

"She's said that a million times before. Then she's gotten into trouble again."

"You sound like you're beating your head against the wall and getting nowhere."

"Is that ever true. I just don't know what to do next. Her sister was a fine student. She's doing well in college. Her younger brother is loved, I mean really *loved* by all of his teachers. Then there's Jill. I keep telling her that if she doesn't graduate she'll be stuck with lousy jobs all of her life, but it doesn't sink in."

"You seem to have an investment in keeping her in school then."

"You're not kidding. Wouldn't you?"

"How about Jill's investment?"

"She's only a child. And not a very intelligent one at that. I'm sure that she'd up and leave given the chance, but I told her that I was going to get her through, no matter what."

"How did she react to that?"

"She told me I was always pushing her."

"Does she feel she's being treated differently than the other children?"

"Yes, she does. She feels I pick on her and not on Larry and Marie. But if I do, it's for her own good and also because they've never given me such problems."

"So she is set apart—even if it is for her own good?"

"Yes. Do you think I'm wrong in doing that?"

"You have her best interests at heart. But there's a difference between that and the results of handling something in a particular way."

"So you think I'm messing it up, don't you?"

"Do you think what you've been doing is helping?"

"No. But I don't know what else to do."

"Well, there seems little else open at this point, but there may be. The important thing to remember is that you are trying to help her, and you're upset because the problem still seems to be present. I guess that's why I get the impression you're willing to try some new strategies with her, and open up possibilities of new goals as well."

"What do you suggest?"

"Nothing other than that we go over the way she views school, you view school, the value your husband sees in it, and the different ways things may turn out and how people would react to them."

The stage is now set for brainstorming, or exploring various approaches to the problem, leaving the possible outcomes open. At this point in the conversation, these factors may be obvious to the counselor, but not to the counselee:

1. Success in school is being pushed by the mother and resisted at some level by the daughter.

2. The daughter is being compared with the other children who are school oriented. Even if she succeeds in getting out of high school it won't be a real success, because the parents will probably respond to the effect that, "Whew, well at least she got out of school. Thank goodness for small favors. Now she's on her own. We did what we could."

3. The mother is oblivious to an alternative such as night high school.

In opening up alternatives, it is not in the best interest of the client to try to convince her that the above points are true. Neither is it appropriate to try to convince the mother to act according to our set beliefs. Taking the opposing view that her daughter need not necessarily finish school this June will accomplish nothing. It will only put us on opposite sides of the fence. Furthermore, going too fast and imposing values on the person can only backfire and cause hard feelings.

The only thing we shouldn't shy away from is an evaluation of the effectiveness of how something is handled by the client. If the person takes personal affront, then this must be questioned. For example, when the mother took offense at the suggestion that alternate approaches *might* be more effective, a differentiation was made between the motivation, which was positive, and the results, which were negative. This differentiation is essential because many people have long equated efforts with intentions and will get upset when we question the effectiveness of their behavior, under the mistaken impression that we are questioning their intentions.

In the case now under discussion, the goals should be to make the daughter's, mother's, and other significant persons' aims explicit. Then the need is to look at other possible outcomes, such as Jill's getting thrown out of school, Jill's leaving school and taking a job, or Jill's going to school at night, etc.

In opening up these areas, if the person balks at discussing them, then this must be brought to the forefront in a non-threatening manner.

"There's no sense in discussing other alternatives. Jill is going to stay in school and that's that."

"Well if you feel that's the only option, I can understand how upset you are—considering the possibility other things might occur."

If the person is not willing to look at alternatives to continuing in school on a full-time, day-school basis, at least you can look at ways in which the mother can take the sting out of the daughter having to stay in school and out of trouble.

In discovering ways to lighten the burden on the daughter, it may be helpful to get the daughter's views via the mother. This can be done by asking the mother to relate the kinds of comments—positive, negative or otherwise—made by the daughter in response to the issue of her continuing in school. Any number of things may be uncovered:

1. The daughter may feel no one says anything to her if school goes well, but if she messes up, they punish her.

2. No one expresses interest in her day other than to say, "How did school go today, Hon? Fine? Oh, that's good."

3. No one gives her future—possibly in a trade or in a clerical position—as much support and positive reinforcement as they give her siblings, who are in college and looking for a "profession."

4. People express surprise when she does well and nod knowingly when she fails.

Bringing these things out in the open can help the person arrive at feasible solutions in conjunction with the counselor.

It is essential to understand that real change takes time and planning. And planning takes specifics. Only after the specifics of the situation are made clear can someone try to implement a new approach or try out new behavior. This may require some role playing with the counselor to see how similar situations might be handled differently. Then the new behavior may need to be tried out with people in the world other than the significant persons who represent the eventual targets of this new mode of acting.

For instance, a planned new approach may start out with a simple question by the counselor to consider how something might be handled differently: "Well, Sue, if you had to do it again, how would you deal with Elyse in this situation?"

Once this question is answered, the same situation could be

approached from different angles: "O.k., so you feel you would have liked to do _____. What's another way you might have handled it?"

Once two or more approaches have been discussed, the old one might be brought back for a look, even though Sue might not have been at all happy with her previous style of acting: "How do you see these two approaches as different from the way you handled it originally?"

After that answer comes out, some prompting could be given to see what some of the benefits were in the original way of acting. After all, people normally act to gain something positive—even if it is only immediate advantage and is a style they *say* they want to replace because it doesn't contribute to a long-range goal: "What do you think was the advantage of the first way of handling it . . . even with all of its stated drawbacks?"

Examining the benefits of old behaviors is essential. The reason is that people must face up to the gain, no matter how small or perverse it is. If they don't recognize it, then they will be tempted to perform the same behavior again, not realizing what the temptation is. They will be caught off guard by the attraction to do what they did in the past, thinking they were past such "useless" behavior.

Counseling goals need to be realistic. They are meant to open up areas for consideration, to accept the person while pointing out apparently ineffective behavior, and to refrain from imposing our own values on those we're interacting with.

The overall goal of counseling is to get people to become self-critical, that is, critical in a way that enables them to evaluate complex factors in a broad, interpersonal situation. Just as it is said, "Give a person a fish and feed them for a day, teach them to fish, feed them for a lifetime," counseling is designed to help people begin to examine their feelings and the style of problem solving they use. In this way, they can become more attuned to how the problems they experience arise, and how they might be prevented or dealt with more effectively.

Chapter 6

Stages of the Interview: A Summary

When we are trying to help someone, we must observe and keep track of many things in the course of the conversation, so a simple organizational guideline that will aid us in keeping things in perspective can be very welcome. Such a guideline will help us direct the conversation productively.

Whether a counseling session is informal or is conducted according to set ground rules in a professional setting, a number of stages are usually involved. They are (1) initial opening, (2) unburdening and looking for key clues, (3) follow-up, (4) brainstorming, and (5) tying it up.

INITIAL OPENING

Our initial contact with a person and the problem being experienced can occur in a variety of ways. The person may call over the phone or be with us in the room when the topic is introduced. It may be brought up immediately or else after a good deal of time has been spent passing pleasantries.

In some cases, the problem may not be brought out in the open until we notice something and give the person an opening. For example, we may get nonverbal signs which prompt us to say something like, "What's the matter, John? You seem sad all of a sudden." Or the person may say something which tips us off to the fact that he wants to discuss something. "From what you're saying, you seem to be really concerned over your son's school problems."

In most instances, though, the topic is brought up directly. Either over the phone, or in person, a clear statement is made to the effect, "I want to talk to you about something."

No matter how the plea is made, the type of initial response we make can have a great impact on the ultimate effectiveness of the interaction. If we express shock, try to avoid going into it with them, or assume our formal "interviewer's voice," we run the risk of shutting off the interaction.

How we react should be governed by the way *we* would like to be treated in a similar situation. Certainly, we would appreciate it if the response included a natural expression of interest in hearing about the difficulty. Then, following the expression of interest and concern, we would probably appreciate some silent space to permit us to unburden ourselves of our general perception of our problem.

UNBURDENING AND LOOKING FOR KEY CLUES

Things have probably been building up in the person prior to his having spoken to us. So after encouraging the person to begin, we should sit back and let him talk. Initially, there may be some problem, but through further encouragement and patient silence, this can generally be overcome.

"The truth is I don't know where to begin. It seems there's so many things involved, and I'm so confused."

"Jim, begin anywhere." (Long pause)
"All right, I guess I might as well start with. . . ."

When the interaction gets going, active listening is the main technique to be employed. We are looking for clues for further exploration, taking note of questions we have, and letting the person open up. Interruption at this stage is only undertaken if there's a genuine confusion on our part as to what the person is saying—confusion to the extent that we would not be able to follow the person any further if we didn't get immediate clarification.

As we saw in looking at the art of questioning (chapter 3), anytime we interrupt someone to ask a point of clarification, we take a risk. By breaking in we may be interfering with the flow of communication at a time when the person may finally be getting to some very sensitive material. So our major goals during the first phase of the contact are to provide an accepting environment within which the troubled individual can open up the floodgates to the topic, to note key points in what the person is saying or how he is saying it, and to note areas for further exploration once the person has completed a general overview of the issue.

FOLLOW-UP

Paying attention to the material initially presented normally raises more questions than it answers. When this occurs, it is natural for the counselor to follow up on what appear to be the important areas and unanswered or partially answered questions.

Selecting the areas is not as difficult an undertaking as might be expected. There's no magic or intuition involved. Just common sense.

In questioning further, the material we need is merely what we would normally require if we were tackling this same problem ourselves. By trying to understand the person's internal frame of reference, while having the advantage of being on the outside of the interpersonal web he or she is caught in, we're in an ideal position to know which areas ought to be looked at further. Moreover, when the person tries to elaborate on techniques which have been tried, we can get an idea of the nuances in the way the problem has been handled.

Often, in the first telling of something, important sensitive details are omitted. When this occurs, we may scratch our heads and wonder what went wrong, because in many cases the outcome seems improbable, given the approach used. By questioning further, by seeking additional data, the nature of the interaction that led to that outcome becomes clearer to *both* the client and the counselor.

> "You say she just blew up and said she didn't want to speak to you again?"
>
> "I couldn't believe it. I just don't know what happened."
>
> "You said you had been just chatting with her and didn't say anything which warranted such a reaction?"
>
> "That's right."
>
> "Well, o.k. Why don't we go back and look at the things you were saying. Maybe we can uncover something that might have ticked her off in some way, without your being aware of it."

In doing this, we have to show we are not trying to trick the person into admitting he or she didn't handle things correctly. We're just looking for the truth. We're trying to perceive the situation from several different vantage points. We're making an attempt to gather *useful* information, not incriminating evidence against those we're counseling.

During the follow-up, we are particularly interested in those same areas we discussed in chapter 3, namely, the specific details of the situation and the feelings the person has about what happened. These feelings should include how the person felt prior to, during, and after the event in question, how he or she felt about what had happened, about the people involved, and about the actions taken in response to the difficulty.

In the example, described in the previous chapter, of the mother who was upset about her daughter's suspension from school, during the initial phase, the counselor just listened to the mother relate her feelings about her daughter, the school, and how her husband didn't handle her daughter correctly when she was younger.

A mental note was made to come back to the school suspension to get a better picture of it. There was no point in doing it when the mother was very upset, and had more of a vested interest in getting how she felt out in the open than in looking more objectively at the situation. However, once the mother had an opportunity to open up, the counselor had a chance to open up the topic of the suspension.

> "You say you were really upset when you heard your daughter was going to be suspended from school?"
> "Yes. I felt like wringing the principal's neck. But there was nothing I could do. I just hope it doesn't keep happening. What a mess!"

Now the counselor can seek to get a more complete view of the situation. The counselor's goal is to find out what happened and how people felt prior, during, and after the event. This process is a necessary prelude to brainstorming, since without a clear understanding of what went on, little can be done in the way of problem solving.

BRAINSTORMING

Brainstorming is that part of the interview in which different ways of handling a problem and their possible results are explored. It occurs only after a fairly complete picture of the factors and feelings involved has been elicited from the coun-selee. Brainstorming is not easy. Although people ask for help, they often resist it because they are afraid to change. Though they want support, they don't want interference. Well-meaning help is often viewed as meddling by the very people who reach out. This is a natural pattern for most of us and should not be viewed as deceptive or hostile.

But even if a counselee seems unwilling to look at alternatives, at this stage of the counseling interview at least other factors can be introduced for consideration. Remember, the goal is not to solve the problem—that may take a lot of time. Rather, it is to introduce new material and open up possible avenues, while supporting the person and accepting their right to feel and do what they think is best. The dialog and discussion on opening up alternatives in chapter 5 elaborates on the handling of this part of the interview.

TYING IT UP

When the end of the contact is approaching, it is a good idea to try to tie things up. During this stage there is a temptation to move quickly to fix everything, to provide advice, rather than sum up what has been covered thus far. It's as though there is a fear that unless something is done now, all will be lost.

Once I was counseling someone with marital problems and I saw the session was drawing quickly to a close. Rather than wait for the next appointment to methodically explore what I was thinking with him, I decided to leave him with some words of wisdom.

One of the problems I assessed was that he didn't seem to be spending enough time out of the house together with his wife. So, rather than waiting until next time to explore why he wasn't aware of the importance of taking her out, I jumped in and said, "Maybe you should go out more often with your wife." He left without saying anything more.

The next time I saw him, he greeted me with the statement: "Well, I took your *advice*." The chills went down my spine, as I responded, "Oh?" "Yeh. I took my wife out for dinner. And while we were out, someone broke into my house and stole my TV."

So much for good advice.

Summarizing things at the end gives a good opportunity to point out things, but it is not the time to make new strides. The end of the session is a fine time to emphasize comments and feelings which the person made with respect to important aspects of his life situation.

In reviewing these feelings and actions, the person gets another chance to see the patterns in a nutshell. The synthesis also provides a presentation of the feelings and factual content together. In this way, there is a greater chance to see the issues for what they are in the person's mind, not merely for what they appear to be on the surface.

Simply following this interviewing structure can be of assistance. People who come for help can benefit if they get a chance to open up and unburden themselves. Even though people resist at some level, they do appreciate our taking time to look at their problems. It is possible for the person to benefit from the contact when we ask questions that reflect their feelings, problem-solve with them, and try to tie things up at the end in somewhat of a summary.

Chapter 7

Some Counseling Guidelines

EVALUATING THE SESSION

An array of feelings can be experienced by us as counselors after a session is over. We can walk away from the contact feeling something positive was accomplished. On the other hand, we can feel ambivalent about the results or be convinced that the whole undertaking went sour.

Particularly when feeling discouraged, there is a need to take stock of the situation so something can be learned from what happened. In the instances where things don't seem to go well, there's a temptation to simply blame the person who came to us. In doing this, nothing positive can result.

If we let our frustrations and bad feelings win out, we probably will think ill of the person and feel a bit disappointed in ourselves. The interaction should actually be looked upon as an opportunity to learn something positive about ourselves and the counseling process. To find out how and why things didn't go as we expected, we should first ask ourselves a number of questions.

Did I expect too much from the interaction in the first place? This is the first question we should ask ourselves. In other words, did I think I could do wonders? Did I expect for some reason that this person would readily give up a lifelong style of dealing with the world? Was there some reason to believe I could fix things up overnight?

Too often we set our goals too high. We expect too much of those we deal with, and see a person's willingness to open up as a sign that she or he will radically alter a familiar approach due to some advice from us.

In the first place, counseling is not advice giving. If people could take advice, they probably wouldn't need to be counseled. Counseling is designed to open up their resources so they can follow their own style of handling things, but in a way that achieves reasonable goals. Secondly, counseling is based on accepting the person as they are without trying to intrude on his or her life style. This is why reflection is a major technique in counseling. So if we are discouraged it may be that we have failed to keep the counseling process in its proper perspective and have expected too much from our work and supportive efforts.

This is the next question we should ask after a seemingly unproductive session. *Did things get worse slowly, or suddenly?* In answering this question we might be able to spot something we said or did which keyed off a negative response in the person. This is helpful to know, not so we can castigate ourselves over our failures, but so we can see what the person is sensitive about, and how we somehow proceeded to unknowingly touch this particular chord.

This self-reflection is important because it allows us to improve our style of working with others. If we can recognize the times when our intervention actually *increases* people's anxiety, we can try to work on it, so the same mistake is not repeated with the person we're working with, or others who may have similar difficulties.

For instance, someone may be talking about her husband in a

derogatory manner. We may initially bolster them by agreeing with them. However, later we may notice that they express guilt over having talked about their husband that way and take steps to correct our stated misconception. Without going into the underlying dynamics of this common occurence, suffice it to say that a counseling principle is: Don't put yourself in a position where you are encouraging someone to be disloyal to their families or friends, because they will feel guilty about it afterwards.

Now even without knowing of this principle, the same conclusion can be arrived at on our own. If we notice a negative outcome when we side with a person against members of their families, then we would try not to jump in and agree with them next time. Instead we should try to get them to talk without our joining in because denunciations of family members usually turn out to be temporary. Rather than focus on the negative aspects of the person's family, we might concentrate on his or her feelings, the possible reasons why the family reacts in a specific way, and how the family may be feeling.

This is only one example of the benefits of pinpointing where a seemingly unproductive interview may have gone wrong, but it serves to illustrate the principle. It takes courage to admit you may have contributed to the negative outcome of the session, but only through this kind of self-reflection will you be able to avoid the same dangers and disappointments in the future.

Since the outcome is not what I would have liked it to be, what do I think of the person now and would I be willing to spend time helping them again? This is the final question which should be asked after an unproductive interaction. This question is important. It brings out in the open our possible frustration and anger regarding the efforts we have spent.

We might be thinking, "What a waste of time! Here she asks for help and all I get is grief from trying to be helpful." However, if we can look at the ways in which we get trapped by the other person, we can be of more use to them and others like them in the future. Also, we can begin to recognize how the people involved in the situation might feel frustrated when they deal with this person.

Don't forget, individuals who are hard to work with don't try to push people away on purpose. They may be ambivalent. Part of them wants to be heard and helped. Another part is afraid of changing and being helped. With patience and a desire to learn from our mistakes, we can continue to work with these types of people, when others have given up. And that's quite an accomplishment in itself!

With these kind of people, it is often difficult not to feel helpless and frustrated. Yet by being willing to listen and by being attentive, we may be helping them more than we realize. There are times when we think we're getting nowhere, but we are closer to the person at that moment than is anyone else in the world.

They may be thinking, "Boy, she has a hard time understanding me, but at least she's interested." Such a half-hearted positive impression in their minds may be the most they can acknowledge, but the fact they even have it is proof that our patience is worth it all.

In going over both the seemingly good, unproductive, and questionable interactions we have with people in distress, we may come up with any number of impressions about how we mishandled something. Though we learn by doing and re-doing, there are a number of counseling techniques and tips worth mentioning. They obviously do not represent the magical key to good counseling. However, if we are aware of some basic helping and interviewing techniques, we can use them to support and facilitate our efforts.

The list of counseling tips we could conceivably cover would be endless. The tips described in this chapter, however, are designed to help people who are beginning their exploration of counseling to make the most of their talents in working with others. The annotated bibliography at the end of the book suggests further readings in counseling, interviewing, and other basic helping techniques.

COUNSELING TIPS

- Pace the conversation according to the needs of the person being helped. Going too fast can be just as bad as going too slow.
- Point out specific reasons for hope. This is much better than giving sugar-coated, general reassurance.
- Point out behavioral patterns that the person exhibits. This can provide insight into his or her complex style of dealing with the world and open it up to easier, more complete examination.
- Question the person when he or she expresses sweeping generalizations or seems to accept illogical thinking patterns regarding himself/herself.
- Maintain an investigative attitude, and use it as a model for people to follow, so they can be their own detectives.
- Don't give advice. Give clear feedback as to what your impressions are of what the person is expressing and feeling.
- Show that you accept the person and the person's right to feel as he or she does. This is not the same as agreeing with present behavior.
- Don't emphasize radical change. Instead, first support the person in pursuing self-examination and in evaluating the factors in the situations presented.
- Be patient. Assimilating new information takes time.

PACING

Each person is unique. How readily someone can assimilate information and confront personal patterns of dealing with the world is quite variable. Furthermore, each person's readiness to deal with these kinds of issues varies from time to time. At times we are ready and anxious to move ahead. Other times, we don't want to face reality. People try to confront us with the truth and we don't want to hear it.

With this variability in mind, as counselors we should attempt to pace the session at a rate comfortable for the person we're dealing with. Going too fast can be just as unproductive as going too slow.

A number of things can tip us off to when we are moving along at too *fast* a pace. The person may be confused about what we are saying. We may be saying things which the person is having great difficulty in accepting. Or the person may quite emotionally demonstrate anger, respond with quick compliance to our interpretation, or become very anxious.

Moving along too quickly can be caused by several factors. In some cases, it might be the counselor's lack of patience with the progress being made and a feeling of futility about the changes occurring. Pacing problems due to impatience and frustration can be handled to a great extent by recognizing the presence of these feelings and not permitting them to govern the course of the interaction. Another step which may help is to remind ourselves regularly of the value of active listening and support of the person, and the unwisdom of hurried intervention on our part.

Another common reason we sometimes behave precipitously is to demonstrate personal expertise. This exhibitionism may show itself in a number of ways. One example of it is when we try to show how well we can interpret what's going on. This attempt to display the possession of a special talent to put things together for the counselee is immature and does not help develop his or her own resources.

Going too *slow* can also be a problem. A person may be anxious to look at personal patterns and styles, and we may hold back. When we hold back, it indicates to the person that we, as counselors, are fearful of proceeding, that, in fact, there is something to be afraid of, embarrassed about, or concerned with. When this occurs we need to take a careful look at our view of the person and the type of material under discussion. Possibly we are underestimating the one we're working with.

Another reason could be we don't really want progress to occur. Let's face it, most of us occasionally like to be in control and tend to be authoritarian with certain types of people. If they are marching ahead without our "precious guidance," they may falter. In fact, the fear is they may realize we're not such great know-it-alls, and that they don't need us as much. One of the aims of counseling is that the other person remain as independent as possible. But at a unconscious level, this may not be what we want. That's why we have to keep a close check on ourselves as counselors.

Problems with pacing in general are due to a lack of appreciation of the resiliency of people, and a lack of awareness of what makes people upset—i.e., of their sensitive zones. Wondering whether you're moving along fast enough is not really a problem. The very people we're working with help us to determine the proper pace. They give us continual feedback as to whether we're moving along at the wrong pace.

When we get the message that we're rushing along or holding up the bandwagon, we should take the opportunity to reflect on why this is occurring and on the feelings we have which prompt such errors. By doing this, we can cut down on the number of times we do it.

If, for instance, we see we are always putting on the "savior" mantel with one type of individual, then we can learn to correct for it and recognize how this kind of person elicits this behavior from us. One of the exciting things about counseling is that the more we try to work carefully with others who are in distress, the more we learn about ourselves. By being sensitive to ourselves as well as to counselees, we can't help but improve our self-examination skills and interpersonal communication talents.

DEALING WITH SPECIFICS

When someone has a problem, frequently friends and family will avoid the issue by responding with very general supportive phrases such as, "Don't worry, everything will be all right" and "You'll see, everything will turn out for the best." When these responses are questioned by the person, they are often followed by more of the same: "How do you know things will work out?" "Oh, they just will. You'll see."

Phrases like these reflect the need of some people to avoid

dealing with an anxiety-producing topic by clamping a sweet lid
on the subject, as quickly as possible. Such generalizations can
also be hazardous to the person's health. Too much support
and reassurance can actually be detrimental because it discour-
ages self-examination and it stifles the pursuit of real solutions
to real problems. Furthermore, if we start pouring on the
syrupy support, the person may start to wonder why we protest
so much. They may start to think perhaps the problem is far
more serious than they ever thought.

Meeting vague negative feelings with amorphous positive
ones is of little value to the person we're dealing with, and
should therefore be avoided. The hope we, as counselors, offer
for the future is based in reality, not sweet dreams. Real hope is
tied to knowing the specifics of the situation. When someone
tells us they are anxious today and don't know why, we just
don't tell them to forget it. We ask them to tell us about their
day. We imply that if they're anxious, there must be a cause.

In response, sometimes we hear, "Nothing unusual happened. I just don't know what it's all about." This response
means nothing. Continued pursuit is in order. "Well, let's go
over what happened and how you felt about things today anyway. Your anxiety has to be caused by something."

One of the important features about the above counseling
response is the inclusion of the word *felt*. It may be that nothing
happened in the outside world to upset the anxious person.
However, something might have keyed off a thought or feeling
about a sensitive area in the person's life. That's why knowing
when a person started feeling the way they do and what they
were thinking and doing prior to the feeling's onset is important
material to elicit.

POINTING OUT BEHAVIORS

As part of our effort to point out specifics, we should try to
focus on behavioral patterns which can provide essential information that might help to short-circuit a problem. For example,

by demonstrating *comparisons* and *contradictions* is what is said, felt, and done, people are able to see where some of their confusion in getting hold of a troublesome issue really lies.

If people report they don't work too hard, but their schedule says they put in sixty hours per week, we have to wonder about the contradiction. If a woman is nice to one sister and nasty to the other, we have to question it. If a male truck driver says no one likes him because he's not college educated, and he has at least three female friends who call him and see him as an interesting man, this whole area of self-image has to be looked at.

By comparing messages and behaviors, or reflecting contradictory ones, we open up the possibility for the other person to reflect on the connections and contradictions, too. By doing this, the person may then be able to view things in a different light and alter how he or she feels about or deals with an issue.

QUESTIONING GENERALIZATIONS

Dr. Albert Ellis has long been a leader in behavioral psychology. One of his approaches to dealing with people is to uncover and replace the illogical thinking patterns they have. Dr. Aaron Beck, a Philadelphia psychiatrist, has done similar work with depressed patients.

Too often, the thoughts we hold get us into trouble. They express beliefs which are myths, false generalizations, and broad sweeping statements which bear little resemblance to reality.

In other words, broad statements like the following would have to be questioned:

"I should be able to be nice to people (i.e., everyone)."

"There's no reason why people (i.e., everyone) shouldn't like me."

"He's my father and he means well, so I shouldn't get angry at him."

Generalizations and superlatives like these need to be exam-

ined carefully. Too often people say things which are not crit-
icized by others because they seem to be only exaggerating.
This may be so, but when such exaggerations are left unchal-
lenged, even though the person saying them doesn't *really* believe what he's saying, they can still have an adverse effect.

So, in the first statement above, the question should be asked,
"Why should you be able to be nice to everyone?" In the next
instance, "What makes you think that everyone should like
you?" And in the next case, "*Anyone* could have done better?"

In the final example, the questioning should be directed at
what occurred between the person and her father. This could
then be followed by exploring the possibility of the feeling being
a natural one, even though it might be one which she is not
happy she expressed.

"How did you happen to get angry at your father?"

"Well, he just kept telling me how skinny I was getting and
that I should eat more. He felt I was neglecting myself, just to
look like a model. He kept harping and harping on it, until I
blew up. Like I said, I really shouldn't have gotten angry. He
only had my best interests at heart."

"I'm confused. You didn't get angry at him because he had
your best interests at heart, did you?"

"No. I got angry because of his harping."

"So, I'm not clear why you're not expected to get angry
when someone harps on something, even if he's your father."

"Well I guess it's to be expected, but I would rather have
controlled myself."

"You might rather have controlled yourself, but would you
agree that it's not so surprising that you got angry, given the
circumstances?"

"Yes, I can see that now. I guess it was sort of natural."

Many times people operate on premises that are based
on philosophical extremes. Many of the philosophies are
ones which are too ideal to be attained completely. They are

designed to provide goals, to provide direction, not to be taken literally."

So, when someone says, "I shouldn't be lazy," or some other such general statement, they have to be questioned. A favorite response of mine to a hasty generalization like the one above is, "Where is it written that you should never be lazy?"

In this case, we're not trying to compromise another's philosophy of life. Rather, we're trying to point to reality. We're trying to recognize that while a person can seek to reach an ideal, he shouldn't castigate himself *as if* everyone else has attained it already and he, the weak one, hasn't. Such a reaction will only lead to despondency and despair, rather than a clear recognition of the factors involved in why he didn't get as far as he originally desired.

GIVING FEEDBACK

In helping others put their behavior in perspective and put to rest absurd thinking, we give feedback, not advice. Advice is direction . . . from *above*. Feedback is reflection from an equal who is trying to consider the issues from a different vantage point.

As counselors, we usually provide little purely new knowledge. Rather, we are involved primarily in questioning the issues from various angles so the person can make a decision regarding what action to take. Given another opportunity to talk with the person, we would problem-solve and imagine how similar situations could be handled in a different fashion in the future. Counselees act on their own. Our goal is not to take over their decision-making powers through the provision of "gems of wisdom." Rather, we act more as a consultant, a nondirective catalyst.

In giving feedback, we are also supporting and modeling a problem-solving, open-ended approach to life's problems. By this I mean that we are encouraging people to be their own

detectives. Self-examination and the determination of the specific circumstances of a situation are encouraged. When we ask
when did it happen, whom were you with at the time, how did
you feel at the time, how did you feel just before and after the
event, etc., we are priming them to ask themselves these same
questions in the future.

SHOWING ACCEPTANCE

By being emphathetic and maintaining a fact-finding
approach, we give people the message that we can accept them
at the same time we question their behavior. Initially, when
questioned or asked to give an illustration of what they mean,
people may take it as an intrusion, or they may be confused, or
feel threatened.

"Do you think I did wrong by the way I handled it?"
"What makes you say that?"
"Well, by the fact you're questioning me on it.'
"No. I just thought we'd get a better look at what went on,
so we could have more of a chance to see why it turned out
the way it did. By questioning, we can get a possibly broader
view of things."

Eventually, when people deal with you enough, they begin to
anticipate the questioning. They'll say something and then go
on to say, "I know. You're going to want an illustration of what
I'm talking about." As people begin to see the questioning as a
way to open up the issues for examination, rather than as a
means to demonstrate wrongdoing on their part, they will provide more information more readily.

As we know, the more comfortable we feel with someone, the
more likely we are to venture out into new sensitive areas of
discussion. Likewise, when we feel the person accepts us and is
interested not in harping on our failings but in working with us
to improve our coping talents, we are more apt to challenge our

old assumptions and make changes in the way we view and act upon things.

EVALUATING FIRST, CHANGING SECOND

Patience and reflection are encouraged in counseling as a first step toward untangling whatever problem the person is facing. When a call for help is made, in most cases there is an implicit belief on the part of the person that *radical* change is needed: "I just can't go on this way. I've got to do something or I'm going to go crazy."

To accept this premise, though, would be a hasty mistake. Radical change—or any major change for that matter—may not, in fact, be needed. A reasonable response to a statement of this sort is to encourage looking at the situation first to see what is actually happening: "Well, let's look at what's going on first. What's happened that made you feel this way?"

By responding in this way, you're putting the emphasis on examining the situation, rather than putting the person on notice that the objective of the two of you working together is to change him or her.

While a person may exclaim, "I've got to change!" and may indeed eventually do so, there is usually a resistance to change, as well. People naturally fear change. We all think to a certain degree "Better the devil we know than the one we don't."

In encouraging people to look at and evaluate the factors involved, we're not trying to fool them until their guards are down so we can zap them with the truth, so they can mend their ways and sweep out the old and bring in the (our) new ways. In fact, in many counseling situations, simply a slightly different perspective on the situation is all that is needed to make a real difference in how the situation is handled. Wisdom, which is the accumulation and mature application of knowledge, recognizes the potency of a minor, but *true*, shift in our train and style of thinking.

Vows of totally changing one's ways by people under stress

are promises made in the wind. They may have impact when they come up in a novel. We may feel confident that Dickens' grumpy, miserly Scrooge meant business when he said, "I shall keep Christmas every day of the year." In real life though, and especially in the counseling environ, big change is not sought after, simply because it may not be needed, or for that matter—possible.

BEING PATIENT

In the cases where some change is required, it will not be accomplished overnight. Assimilation of new material, and trial-and-error learning, takes time.

Think of how long it takes us to change our minds. Even in a discussion with other "flexible, open-minded people," amending an opinion of our own can be a big deal. We can be stating our arguments and hearing better ones presented by someone else, but we'll still hold on to our viewpoint . . . at least temporarily, for we don't want them to know they're right and we, heaven forbid, are wrong.

The same is true with those we try to help. There is an understandable resistance to accepting new pieces of information which don't fit established habits of thinking. Also, since learning is a gradual process, we can't expect people to change behavior both quickly and effectively.

Reflection, practice, questioning, thinking about new behavior, and chancing a new style of action takes time. Old behavior was not born overnight and it won't be replaced in a short span of time either.

With an awareness of the counseling process and employing the tips noted here, the problems people have won't seem so overwhelming to them, or to us as counselors. An important key in using them though—and forgive me for emphasizing this so much, but it is so important—is not to expect miracles. To do so could be disastrous—not to mention fruitless and frustrating.

In counseling, half the battle is won when we don't expect too much, but rather, through the use of commonsense techniques, accept the possibility of accomplishing something positive . . . namely, giving a person in distress the message that someone will listen to them and work as an equal with them in trying to get a handle on the problem in question. What more can another person ask of us, or we of ourselves?

Chapter 8

Common Problems: Depression, Anxiety, and Stress

Problems, like people, come in almost every shape and size imaginable. To catalog a majority of them here, or to describe them in the context of certain stages of life, would be a fruitless and unnecessary undertaking. What would have to be compacted into one chapter has already been given more than adequate treatment in existing volumes (for example, Gail Sheehy's *Passages*). Instead, this chapter will discuss a number of common complaints often confronted by people in daily life, namely depression, anxiety, and stress.

Particular problems may be varied, but generally it is sadness, insecurity, or tension that we are asked to deal with in our neighbors, family members, and colleagues. They come in and say, "Boy, am I jittery. What am I going to do?" Or they look glum and report, "I just feel down all the time. I can't continue to go on like this." Or, "I feel so tense all the time; I'm under such stress. Yet, I can't seem to get out from under it all."

There are specific difficulties we may encounter in working with people with these kinds of problems. There are also a number of basic approaches which can be used to get beyond the affect (mood) and uncover the factors causing the negative emotions. The debilitating aspects of depression, anxiety, and stress will be presented with an eye to arriving at a better understanding of their causes and treatment. This practical information will help prevent us from being overwhelmed by other people's emotional distress, which will in turn enable us to provide support and assistance to those who seek our help.

WHO GETS DEPRESSED?

Say the word "depression," and the idea of sadness usually comes to mind. We frequently identify sadness through a person's facial expression. If someone is crying, for instance, we feel it must be because this individual is depressed, and we seem to key our diagnosis of whether people are down or not to what their faces say. Facial expression, though, is only one clue to depression. Depression is actually a mood state with a multitude of degrees and characteristic symptoms. Depression is neither a new problem, nor rare. We have all experienced mild forms of depression, which we describe as being "down," "blue," "sad," "black," "in the pits," "in a funk," or any other number or other terms which convey our being at a low ebb. Depression can be troublesome, even when it isn't severe. When feeling even slightly down, a woman at home taking care of her family can begin doubting her overall sanity and purpose in life. During a case of the "blahs," an executive may find it hard to concentrate or produce at work.

No age group is exempt from feelings of depression. Children and older adolescents may experience periods of prolonged grief or depression. During such periods, their responses may be personally or externally destructive. In Japan and Germany, when students find out they can not go on to college because they have failed to qualify in the highly competitive system, suicide is sometimes seen as a way out. When depression hits younger children, apathy in school may affect their grades, or anger aimed at combating their feelings of sadness and immobilization may produce destructive behavior.

Wealth is by no means a guarantee against depression, be it wealth of knowledge or of financial resources. Though some have joked, "I'd rather be rich and depressed than poor and depressed," the number of financially well-off people in despair is no laughing matter. The powerful are not exempt from depression's devastation either. Winston Churchill, for example, experienced recurring depression, which he referred to as his "black friend." Abraham Lincoln experienced such marked drops in mood he feared carrying a gun in case the temptation to commit suicide might be too great to resist.

Depression can be present in any type of person—rich, poor, young, elderly, Caucasian, Chicano, unemployed, business executive, politician, religious leader. No group is exempt. The picture is even more extensive when including depression in its mildest form. All of us have had periods when we've been unusually down emotionally, unable to respond to things adequately, and generally incapable of functioning optimally. Other people might have noticed it. We might have tried to shake it, but the feeling and its concomitant effects stuck with us more than we'd care to admit.

Various types of difficulties can precipitate depression, and many of us are predisposed to its onset. It is important, then, to look at some of the symptoms of mild (nonpathological) depression, the kinds of things which might produce its onset, and what we might expect in dealing with a person experiencing minor depression. Factors relating to severe (pathological) depression will be discussed in the chapters on crisis intervention (9) and obtaining professional help (11).

SIGNS OF DEPRESSION

Most of us are familiar with a number of signs of depression. Yet other signs are not so familiar because on first blush they may not appear to be related to depression. To ensure such clues are not missed, you should attempt to answer a number of questions when dealing with persons seeking help. Not only will answering these questions help rule out or uncover the possibility of depression, but it may produce information which will be of help no matter what the problem is.

RECOGNIZING DEPRESSION

- How does the person feel emotionally?
- Is the person reporting any vague physical ailments?
- Does the person's mental or physical energy seem to be at a low ebb?
- Is the person sleeping all right and is he or she eating well?
- Is the person drinking more alcohol, taking more medication, or smoking cigarettes or marijuana more than usual?
- How does the person feel about himself?
- Does the person express fantasies of escaping or getting out of the situation?

How does the person feel emotionally? The answer to this question can be quite varied. Someone can be upset, feeling blue, angry, agitated, happy, O.K., blah, worried, fearful, excited, or any other number of things. To answer this question and determine what the person's mood level is, we should ask the person to report personal feeling levels, or we should point out our observations ("You seem really down"). This should enable us to start an open discussion in this area. As emphasized in earlier chapters, the very process of pointing out the obvious and setting up an accepting milieu in which someone can vent and discuss their feelings can be helpful in itself.

When someone opens up we usually can get some idea of the severity and persistence of the depression. If the problem is so severe that the person is thinking of killing himself, or the problem has been present for so long that it's affecting the person's overall effectiveness, then professional help is obviously warranted—and *quickly!* Sometimes the severity of depression is difficult for the nonprofessional to ascertain, so when there is any doubt, be supportive, but also help get the person to see a professional.

If the depression is not extreme, the person can talk about it, and can express some anger along with the depression, then we can probably facilitate the person's coming to grips with it. Our help might include being supportive through patient listening, questioning the person as to the details surrounding the feelings of being "down," and pointing out why you think this un-wanted feeling will pass. (Thinking that there will be a time when they will feel better will help the person deal with their temporary depression.)

Is the person reporting any vague physical ailments? Sometimes mild depression is masked by the presence of vague physical symptoms. Headaches, stomachaches, cold symptoms, or feel-ing sore all over may point to a psychological ache as well. While we obviously shouldn't play physician with people, such physical complaints can tip us off to the possible presence of emotional ailments as well. Emotional depression and minor physical ailments are often present simultaneously. Asking whether they have discussed the generally poor way they feel with a physician can open up the topic. Sometimes people have avoided discussing their general malaise with their doctor and may be willing to talk about it now.

Is the person sleeping and eating well? Sometimes the person's sleeping and eating habits are upset by feelings they have. A change in appetite or sleeping habits can indicate that some-thing is awry and can give us a basis for asking what's going on and when they noticed the change.

"I just can't seem to sleep right and I'm losing weight I can't afford to lose."

"What do you mean you can't seem to sleep right?"

"Well, I just toss and turn trying to get to sleep. And when I finally do fall asleep, I only wind up getting up again at three or so. Then the process begins again with me trying to fall asleep, but instead just ending up tossing and turning again like earlier in the evening."

"What do you think about when you toss and turn?"

"I wind up worrying and thinking through everything."

"That's not unusual. I think we all go through that when there are a few things which are particularly on our mind. What specific things do you think about?"

If the person in the above instance was eating too much or too little without the presence of a sleep disturbance, the same questioning procedure could be followed. In other words, the person could be asked what he or she was thinking about when eating his way through several cans of deluxe mixed nuts. In this way, the person can focus on the issues which appear to be a problem, and an opportunity for support and problem-solving can be created.

Some people, of course, are forever losing sleep or stuffing themselves in an attempt to short-circuit the depression or agitation. We all handle things in different ways, so if someone who is generally successful in life has a habit like this, the only thing he or she might need at times of particular stress is our warm attentive listening and encouragement. Expecting someone to change a whole life-style in such instances would be unrealistic.

How does the person feel about himself? Depression and low self-esteem go hand in hand. Knowing what the person's self-image is and what current coping skills are can be an eye opener for both the counselor and counselee. How people cope with stress is an important indicator of their self-image and how good they feel about themselves at a given point in time. People who are down about themselves and life may exhibit poor coping skills and may see few or no ways out of their difficulty. An assessment of the person's self-image and ability to cope can point to the presence of depression and also to its cause.

PHYSICAL CAUSES OF DEPRESSION

The reasons why people get depressed are numerous. Basically, though, the causes of mild depression can be divided into physiological and psychological ones.

The major physiological factors involved in depression are nutrition, drugs, and sleep. Our bodies run on food. When we don't eat properly, part of the outcome can be a lowering of our mood level. How we feel has a lot to do with our nutritional intake. At the end of a long day in which we only grabbed a snack here and there, we may feel "down" partly because of a nutritional deficiency.

Drugs may also affect our body and mood level. Alcohol is a depressant. Initially it may make us feel good, relax us. However, the morning after might produce a hangover due to excessive intake and a slight emotional depression as well. The depression is due not only to the guilt we might feel about having had a bit too much, but also to a chemical response to the alcohol intake itself. Drugs other than alcohol can also produce depression, particularly during the period immediately after the drug ceases acting on the system. This applies to prescribed as well as unprescribed drugs.

When we use drugs or alcohol during those times when we don't have enough sleep or proper food, we may be starting a vicious cycle. For while they can produce mood changes, the very changes they incur can lead to further sleep loss, inadequate food intake, and drug abuse, as a means of avoiding the depression. This is why getting one's proper rest and maintaining a proper diet is important. Also, it is part of the reason why drug abuse, including alcoholism, can be difficult to cure. The drugs induce the depression and are also used to prevent the person from facing the causes of it, while altering the person's mood.

DEALING WITH HELPLESSNESS

Psychological causes for depression are probably more numerous than the physical ones. Yet, for our purposes we shall deal with only two of the broader ones: helplessness and anger.

Helplessness occurs when our coping mechanisms appear temporarily out of order. This can occur for any number of reasons. A situation may be very new to us and we are temporarily overwhelmed. We may have reached a point in our lives where we need to alter our goals. We may need to be a little more patient with others, ourselves, and the situation: *when* we do something is just as important as what we do. The potential causes of helplessness go on and on.

There are a number of things we can do for people once we observe that the feeling of helplessness is a central issue. Among them are:

Demonstrate a willingness to listen to their concerns about being ineffectual.

Help them achieve goal clarification.

Participate in a problem-solving operation.

Provide support for the belief that things will improve (if, in fact, this is true).

Show a desire to look at current thinking patterns.

The two vignettes below show how a friend or colleague can help a person who feels helpless and depressed. In the first of these, a father has just learned his son has a learning disability and is talking to his boss about it.

"A learning disability! I knew Jeff was having problems, but I didn't think it was anything serious. I thought he'd grow out of it. Now, I don't know. I feel so helpless. I'm not sure whether it's something he inherited from us, or has to do with how we treated him. I don't even know what kind of treatment he needs, how long, or how expensive it will be. I just never thought one of my children would become retarded."

"The school didn't say he was retarded. From what you've told me, they indicated he had some type of disability in learning."

"Well, isn't it the same thing?"

"I don't know. I'm in advertising, not psychology; but there are ways you can find out. What do you plan to do in this respect?"

"You think I should find some educational center or school psychologist?"

"Maybe eventually. Isn't there someone locally you could speak to about it and some place within reach where you could get a basic book about it? It seems your goal is to familiarize yourself with what's involved, no?"

"I guess so. I probably should start at the school. I only heard about Jeff from my wife this morning; the school called her. We should probably set up an appointment with the school, see the teacher and maybe the school psychologist, if necessary. Also, I guess I can drop in at the paperbook bookstore on the first floor of the building. They might have something on it. I'll be glad, though, when I know something more definite."

"It sounds that way. When you first hear these things and it's close to home, it's natural to be upset and worry about what's wrong and what's the best thing to do. After you take the steps you've outlined, though, then you'll know more about what the situation is and what you need to do. You'll have a better handle on it."

Another example of temporary helplessness, and a style of intervening in such a case, is illustrated in the following instance of someone who's having a problem finding employment. In this typical situation, a young woman is speaking with her father.

"What's the matter, Hon?"

"You wasted your money, Dad. You wasted one big chunk of your money."

"So what else is old?"

"No, I'm not kidding."

"What are you talking about?"

"Sending me to school. It was all a waste."

"Having a hard time with finding a job, eh?"

"I've been pounding the pavement. I'm sick of it. It's the same old garbage. Each job I apply for requires previous experience. How are you supposed to get experience if you can't get a job? I think I was born too late. I should have come along when they were giving positions away."

"I don't quite remember those days."

"You know what I mean. This is serious. What am I going to do? The situation really seems hopeless."

"What kind of positions are you looking for?"

"*Anything.* Believe me, anything!"

"When we feel hopeless and a bit desperate, it's natural to feel the way you do. I can understand and accept it, Carol; but it won't help you to get a job."

"Then what do you suggest?"

"Before I go into the suggestion business, let's see why you feel so hopeless. I think that's one of your main stumbling blocks. You're already very upset and feel all is lost."

"I just can't help it."

"What do you mean?"

"Well I've tried so many things. I'm just ready to give up. That's all."

"Well, sit down. Let's see what you've tried. "Tell me what you've been doing to get a job."

"Well, I listed myself with the college placement bureau. I told them I was interested in a job in advertising. Then I've answered ads in the paper for ad assistants, but without any luck. Finally, out of desperation, I went to three employment agencies and they said all they had were secretarial positions. Finally, I started knocking on doors of companies in the city to see if anything was open. The result: a big fat zero. So, what else am I supposed to do? I really think I've done all I can."

"What made you decide on advertising?"

"Well, my major is in English. I can't think of any other

interesting field where I could use it. In desperation, though, I told the agencies I would do anything, so it's not as though I'm not open to suggestions."

"And they responded?"

"Well, they said I was unskilled, so I would have a hard time finding something."

"So, on the one hand, you looked for advertising jobs, but when things didn't seem to be open, you told potential employers you would work in any area."

"You think that was a mistake?"

"Well, it seems on the one hand you're looking for a very specialized position, and on the other you are possibly giving them the impression you don't know what you want to do."

"Well, what do you think I should have done?"

"I don't know. I'm not an English major. However, it would seem there would be someone who could help you narrow down the types of jobs and traineeships you might apply for, given your broad background."

"Like who?"

"Are there people in your school, either in the English department or the placement or guidance office, who can be of help?"

"There might be, but I doubt it."

"But it's one avenue of approach, eh?"

"Yes, I guess you're right. Still, I think I'm going to need a contact the way the job market is today, no matter what you say."

"What makes you think I don't feel that the idea of a contact is a good one?"

"Didn't you just say I should go to the school and ask them for help?"

"Right, but I think your ideas will turn out to be the best. You know your situation better than anyone. I believe, however, you would do best to approach the job problem on a number of fronts. After all, didn't you say getting a job was going to be a problem?"

"A killer."

"Fine. So, you go to the school. We'll sit down and discuss what contacts we might have in the family and among our friends later tonight when your mother's home from work."

"But we don't know anyone in advertising, do we?"

"Probably not, but we may know people in allied areas— ones suggested by people at your school—which may give you a start. Remember, if you take a position, it doesn't have to be one you're so thrilled with you have to stay in it all of your life. After all, the experience is an issue; they're big on it in business even if it's in a related area."

"I hadn't thought of that. You know, I feel a bit better. At least I have a few things to work on. Maybe something will turn up."

"I'm glad you feel better. We'll do everything in our power to make something turn up. We'll look at a number of options to see what is really open to you without being too specialized or general, o.k.?"

"Sure. Thanks a lot."

In both examples, the listener set the atmosphere in a way that it was relaxed and open. The person in each case felt it was all right to vent their frustrations and feelings of impotence. When this was done, an effort to clarify immediate goals and develop steps for solving the problems at hand were undertaken. Finally, after the airing of feelings and mutual problem-solving, a look was taken at the person's current thinking patterns.

As can be seen, there's nothing magical in helping someone. But neither were these interventions mere purposeless interaction that anyone could do. In a brief conversation, for instance, the busy employer might have been tempted to jump in early in the game and give the person a sugar-coated pep talk: "Hey, don't worry, things will work out. It may be nothing." The implication of such a response is, "I don't want to listen to this; it makes me feel uncomfortable and helpless. Please go away and get back to work . . . come back when things are better so I can say, 'See, I told you things would work out.'"

In light conversation, where people don't involve themselves in problem-solving with the person in need, the temptation is to provide a pat solution. In giving pat solutions, though, we risk taking away the independence of the other individual and it seems like we're trying to push the way we would deal with it. This usually fails to be of any help to the person because people are different and have different goals and styles of coping.

In the conversation between father and daughter, the father also demonstrated ideal helping skills. First, he had a good deal of patience with his daughter. Not only did he encourage her to open up, but he did not snap out when she expressed irritability and a sense of global futility about what they were talking about. Neither did he march in paternally and attempt to offer the golden key to solving the problem. Rather, he sought to work with her on developing her own avenues of approach.

As in the first example, in tying down the problem to specific approaches, the person's overall feeling of helplessness started to diminish. There was hope—hope based on the perception that there is a way out. This is very important, since people often feel they have tried everything and the situation is generally hopeless, with no real way out unless a break comes along or something happens to them.

This passive waiting for something to happen can become quite serious. It is based on the belief that the person can't do anything or initiate actions, and it encourages a passive outlook. A vicious circle can result if someone doesn't have the patience to demonstrate a belief in the person's coping powers while problem-solving with them.

The emphasis in dealing with the depressed person who feels helpless is on *patience*. Depressed people can be most irritating. They seem to want help, but when we reach out, they may seem to indicate that our efforts on their behalf are foolish. This can arouse a good deal of anger in us if their resistance is not anticipated and pointed out in a nonangry way.

The best way to deal with the potential resistance is to keep in mind a number of points prior to and during your interaction with the person. These points can be summarized as follows:

1. We can help them most by being patient, supportive, and not quickly dismissing their expressions of helplessness and anger.

2. In most cases, the real difficulty lies not so much in the problem they bring up, but rather in their *perception* of the problem and the negative way they view their coping abilities. Therefore, we shouldn't try to jump in and solve the problem, but methodically support a renewed, sensible effort on their part to handle it.

3. Just because people don't leave us feeling super does not mean we've failed to help them. To think so might make us not want to try to help them in the future, when, in fact, this would be the worst thing we could do. If we are willing to accept people's right to feel down at times, they will recognize this and come back with renewed hope that someone cares.

4. Depressed people are often down because of erroneous, all-encompassing messages they give themselves. "There's nothing I can do," "I feel so futile," "I guess I'll just have to wait until something happens" are all global negative messages. Part of the effort we make with depressed people centers around questioning these messages. Ask them why a particular failure means there's nothing they can do in a situation, or why they see a particular bit of bad luck as evidence that their whole life is going wrong. Point out the absurdity of such expectations and thinking patterns, and then have the person go over the steps they've taken in the situation and the feelings they've had.

DEPRESSION AND ANGER

Pent-up anger is another major psychological cause of depression. People sit on their anger for any number of reasons, and when they do, it can lead to feelings of remorse, ineffectuality, and self-deprecation. Recognizing the anger and identifying the reasons for it is an important step in helping the depressed person. The tip-off to the presence of such anger is when the person seems to assume all of the responsibility for a problem. The following conversation shows how anger can be recognized and examined.

"What's the matter, Toni?"

"I just can't seem to handle Mom. She's been so good to me all these years, but I find that I treat her horribly. She's so sweet. Her treatment of me and the kids is all in my best interest and theirs, but I get so upset with her. I wish I wouldn't blow off the handle that way."

"What's been going on recently between the two of you?"

"Well, last night I told the boys they could stay up another half-hour. I really didn't think they should have, but they were being good and I'd rather they sit and watch TV quietly than fight in their bedroom."

"And?"

"Well, when Mom walked in she told them to go to bed and she started hounding them. They got upset. Then she came to me and told me I was spoiling them and that they had answered her back, so I had no choice but to punish them by sending them to bed. What a mess. Well, at any rate, I told her I was tired of her meddling and she got angry at me and stormed up to bed. I went up and apologized, but she wouldn't even talk to me. When Jack finally came home from the evening shift, I was all in tears. He got angry at me *and* my mother, and well it just made the whole thing worse. I'm just a failure with everyone it seems." (Crying)

"You seem really down on yourself."

"Well, I never seem to do anything right. I guess I do spoil the kids, and I don't raise them as well as mother could, but I do my best."

"What does Jack think?"

"He thinks I should tell my mother off, but I love her. I'm bad enough to her as it is. I ought to be nicer."

"You say you're bad to her. Can you explain how you were bad to her in the incident last night?"

"Well, I shouldn't have told her to stop meddling. They are her grandchildren. And she was right."

"How were you feeling when you told her to stop meddling?"

"I was angry, I mean annoyed that she got them worked up."

"So you were angry because you felt she got them worked up?"

"Well, I realize I'm wrong in that now. She was right, of course. I do spoil them."

"That's another issue. You were angry at her because she got them worked up. How did that occur?"

"Well, as I said. I had told them one thing and she then told them another, and they got upset and confused."

"Do you think that's good for them?"

"No. I guess that's what bothers me. I don't think it's good for them to have more than Jack and I telling them what to do, especially after I've told them one thing and she tells them another. They're losing respect for me and I'm losing control of them."

"So, you were angry at your mother for interfering. Even if she has the children's best interest at heart, you were thinking they're your children and you're responsible for raising them."

"Yes, but she means well."

"A lot of people who mean well make mistakes."

"But I don't want her to think I don't love her."

"What would make her think that?"

"Well, if I get angry at her, wouldn't she feel that way?"

"Well, you continue to get angry at her now because you don't believe she should interfere with the way you raise your children. But you don't express it when you're calm—only after a problem has occurred. Instead of letting the resentment build, how do you think you could tell your mom not to give your children orders countermanding yours?"

"That's just it. If I say something about her interfering, she gets hurt. Nothing I say seems right."

"Well, it seems you tell her only when you're distraught. Also, maybe your mother needs to be told constantly until it gets through. Otherwise, it seems your children will continue to suffer and so will you and Jack."

"But she'll feel I'm blaming her for all my problems."

"Are you?"

"No. Though sometimes I feel we'd be better without her meddling."

"If you feel that way then you must be angry at her interference. You also must be convinced she is causing problems."

"I am."

"Then you have to talk to her to at least open the question. If you're afraid of her rejection of you because of it, then recall your priorities and the goal you have in bringing up the topic with her."

"What do you mean?"

"Well, you and your husband have the responsibility to raise your children, just as your mother had the responsibility for raising you and your brothers. This doesn't mean you're rejecting your mother, but rather you are setting things straight. Also, if you let her know how you feel when you're not angry yourself, she can't accuse you of trying to lash out at her. If she does, then it's her problem. Since she is your mother you can help her with it, but not at the expense of your children."

"That's easier said than done."

"That's right, but it's a beginning."

The above interaction has been compressed for purposes of space here. In reality, Toni would do a lot more of the talking and the helper would be a good deal less directive. However, this vignette does show a number of points on dealing with a depressed person who is trying to hide or suppress the anger present.

The anger must be opened up to see why it isn't coming out more directly. In Toni's case it may be because she fears rejection by her mother and at the same time doubts her ability to raise her children. In addition, she may bottle up her anger because she fears that expressing it directly would be so devastating that she might do something outrageous that she would regret. The goal is to get the anger out in the open to show that it is there. The next step is to demonstrate that one doesn't have to deal with an unsatisfactory situation out of anger, but that reasonable measures can be taken in the hope of improving the situation for all concerned.

One factor in people's inability to deal with anger in a healthy way is their confusion of assertion and aggression. Many people think that if they experience anger and act on it, that they are behaving aggressively and that others will think ill of them for it. But it is possible to recognize anger and then act in a calm, assertive way that is intended to help a situation. By helping people sort out the difference between anger, aggression, and assertion in the actions they take, the purposes they have, and the way they handle others (who themselves may mistakenly equate assertion with aggression) it's possible to help people deal with their problems more directly.

ANXIETY IN DAILY LIFE

Throughout classical Greek literature we see references to the sin of "hubris" (excessive behavior). To the Greeks of that era, excess in any form was wrong. They constantly emphasized and encouraged all to live in line with the golden mean. Hubris refers to excesses in either direction. Too *little* was just as bad as too much; starvation and gluttony were equally horrible.

Anxiety works the same way—too little can be as bad as too much. If we're overly anxious, we will suffer notably. On the other hand, if we feel no anxiety whatsoever about our current efforts and future aspirations, our motivation would probably shrivel and dry up.

Anxiety has a place in our lives. However, the role it plays is a precarious one. If it becomes too predominant, it stifles the very activity it would normally facilitate. This has been shown to be the case among college students preparing for exams. When almost no anxiety is present, the student is not apt to prepare well. Slight anxiety regarding performance on a test is a positive factor. When students are a bit worried about how they will fare, they tend to work harder to ensure good results. When the anxiety becomes too great though, the motivation to study becomes thwarted. The student who is very worried about the outcome becomes so upset that the worrying interferes with his studying. Efforts at mastering the material are supplanted by feelings of, "What's the use; I'll never get it now. It's too late!"

The same phenomenon can be expected in any area of life. We are surrounded by people with anxiety problems, on occasion we fall prey to this condition ourselves.

Joan was someone who was overly anxious. She had moved into a new neighborhood with her husband and a four-month-old baby. She was so anxious to make new friends that she was sugar sweet to everyone she met. The house was always filled with four or five of the neighbors' children, whom she constantly invited to stay for dinner. She was under constant tension and dreaded people coming over because she thought she might make a mistake and say something wrong. Also, her husband was ready to pull his hair out because the house was always in an uproar—even during mealtime—due to the presence of other people's children.

Bill had the opposite problem—little anxiety and even less motivation. He started his new job at a management consultant firm and appeared to show great promise. His credentials seemed to be impeccable. However, he never seemed too excited about the job. He had come from a large corporate setting and this small growing firm seemed below him—even though the money was better here. He felt the job would be a snap and that he could teach them a lot and in turn would learn nothing. His superiors noticed his lax outlook from the beginning.

Though they were impressed by his knowledge, they thought he seemed to lack the motivation to work hard enough to actualize his potential. In essence, he was missing the requisite anxiety about his performance to produce adequately. He was asked to leave after five months.

Sharon experienced a very disabling kind of anxiety. She wanted to go back to school, get a master's degree in business administration, and get a part-time position. However, she dreaded talking to her husband about it because she felt he would disagree vehemently and feel threatened by her suggestion to do something so independent. Consequently, anytime she would get ready to broach the topic she would become quite anxious. Physically her mouth would get dry, she would start to sweat, her heart would start beating rapidly, and she would become nauseous. These physical reactions would become so unpleasant that she would put off discussing it.

CAUSES OF ANXIETY PROBLEMS

The causes of too little anxiety include overconfidence, a denial of anxiety (manifesting itself, for example, as a show of bravado by a person who finds feelings of insecurity too unbearable), ignorance of the complexity or demands of a situation, and apathy. Apathy usually results from previously unrewarding experiences concerning the anxiety-provoking situation. The person may have tried everything to ward off his or her anxious feelings and met with no results, or the person may have been so overanxious that withdrawal seemed the only reasonable alternative.

Too much anxiety can usually be attributed to something real or imagined which stirs up fears of loss of control, retaliation, physical injury or separation. A person who fears losing control is afraid that "letting go" will result in aggressive or antisocial behavior. Jane, for instance, was constantly anxious around her mother. Her counselor finally determined that Jane was fearful of losing control and acting out physically against her mother, and that she was also afraid of being beaten up by her mother. Due to her concern about loss of control, she constantly avoided any constructive criticism of her mother and behaved in a very constricted manner when around her. Anxiety due to fear of retaliation occurs when we do something which makes us feel guilty. Though most of us feel guilty sometimes about some of the things we do, occasionally the guilt becomes exaggerated and we feel very uncomfortable. This kind of guilt can paralyze us for a period of time and waste valuable energy.

Anxiety about physical injury is tied to early childhood fears. When anxiety about physical harm is not present at all, or is subject to massive denial, people take unwarranted and dangerous risks in life. When this fear is too great, people become so conservative that they take no chances at all. Such people avoid moves of any sort, even the smallest in nature. They avoid change and revel in the status quo.

The final anxiety-producing category is fear of separation. Once again, if the childhood has been a healthy one, then an actual or anticipated interpersonal loss can usually be dealt with successfully. If a woman is feeling blue two weeks after her husband of forty years has died, it is a natural way of dealing with her loss. However, if a woman in her early twenties is still pining for a young man she knew for only two weeks, three years ago, then naturally there is a problem centering around separation.

COPING WITH ANXIETY

All of us have to deal with anxiety-producing situations every day. If our anxiety were unbridled in all cases, we would never be able to accomplish anything. Therefore, we manage to keep the anxiety in check through the use of various coping mechanisms.

One of the ways we cope is through consciously avoiding a situation. We may walk across the street when we see someone who usually manages to upset us, or we may put thoughts which make us uneasy out of our mind. Most of us develop certain habits to help us avoid dealing with things which make us anxious. Smoking and overeating are two common responses. The advantage of these kinds of mechanisms is that they are observable and more within our control. For instance, if we notice that we eat when we're upset, we can spot the pattern and try to stay away from the loaded refrigerator.

The unobservable devices we use to deal with anxiety are referred to generally as "defense mechanisms." Some of these mechanisms are well known and are mentioned by us all in daily life. If a person seems to be making excuses for her or his behavior without knowing it, we call it "rationalization." When we get angry at a person when we should really be expressing our anger at someone else, we call it "displacement." Since these mechanisms are not readily observable, control is not as easy to accomplish without help.

When defense mechanisms are used infrequently and in an unexaggerated fashion, no one really takes notice. When they are used in a somewhat exaggerated fashion occasionally, we term it defensiveness. When a person seems to be chained to the use of defense mechanisms, when their usage interferes with effective adaptation in life, and when people readily notice the person has a problem, we generally refer to the pattern as "neurosis."

COUNSELING ANXIOUS PEOPLE

Neurotic individuals require professional help, but there are a whole host of temporarily defensive or anxious people who could benefit from some caring, friendly counseling. There are numerous instances in which family members, business colleagues, peers, and friends are anxious about something and want to chat about it with us.

The two major mistakes to avoid on such occasions are jumping in too quickly with reassurance and allowing ourselves to get trapped by the other person's anxiety. Quick reassurances did nothing to alleviate the obvious anxiety felt by Dan, who was admitted to a psychiatric inpatient unit after he had a bad LSD trip. Initially he seemed quite disoriented, frightened, and incoherent. The next day he seemed alert, quiet, and tense. During his first meeting with the staff, the workers were trying to allay his anxiety by telling him everything was going to be all right now that he was in the hospital, but he still looked like a frightened bird. Finally, one of the staff, who had just entered the room after completing an emergency consultation elsewhere in the hospital, said quite directly, "My goodness, you look scared as heck." At this, Dan started to cry and admitted he was afraid he was going crazy. Following this, there was a discussion of his specific fears, which were dealt with in detail rather than in a pat, syrupy fashion.

Getting caught up in the other person's anxiety is another pitfall to avoid. Anxious people may tend not to hear what we're saying, they may project their anger onto us at the same time that they're reaching out to us, or they make us anxious through the way they act or through their expressions of nervousness. If we can keep our own feelings in check and try to support the person while attempting to tie their anxiety to something concrete, the results can be quite positive, as shown in the following example.

"I'm glad you weren't out when I called. I really wanted to come over and chat."

"You look really jumpy, Dawn."

"I just haven't been myself lately. I don't know what it is."

"When did you start feeling this way?"

"Oh, I don't know . . . Sunday."

"While I'm making the coffee, why don't you tell me about it."

"There's nothing to tell. It started all of a sudden."

"Well what was happening last weekend?"

"Nothing much. On Saturday, John and I went out to look at houses, like we have for the past two months. We went out with the Weinsteins at night, and Sunday we sat around reading the papers. Later in the afternoon, John had to go in; he had an emergency at the hospital. Then early in the evening I started getting jittery. Here it is Tuesday, and I still feel crummy."

"What happened while John was gone?"

"Nothing. I finished reading a couple of sections of the *Times*, did a few things and took a look at the house plans we got the day before."

"What kinds of things were you thinking about, Dawn?"

"Nothing much, just about the house plans and some of the things I had read. . . ."

"How do you feel about moving?"

"It's no big deal. It might be for *you*, but for John and me, it's not. We've been ready for it for years."

"But that doesn't answer my question; how do you feel?"

"About moving?" (Long pause)

"Well, I'm looking forward to it actually." (She then relates all of the advantages of moving. However, in doing so, she doesn't seem very pleased about the prospect—the tone in her voice and her facial expression seem to say something else.)

"There seems to be a lot of advantages to moving. There seems to be an expression on your face, though, that says you have some other feelings about it."

"Well, sure I do. You've never made a move like this. I'm sure you would have even more doubts, given your sheltered background, so why shouldn't I have doubts?"

"That's the point; why shouldn't you?"

"Well, I do, of course." (She then relates her doubts. After them, her friend asks her what her husband thinks about the move and the area is opened up enough so she can see how the move is affecting her feelings and producing some anxiety.)

In the above illustration, the neighbor had to keep calm in the face of subtle and not-so-subtle assaults by her anxious friend. Yet by doing this she was able to help draw her out so she could discuss the anxiety-provoking aspects of moving, see that they were quite natural, and realize that it was unnecessary to keep them boxed up inside.

Anxious people, like depressed people, are often some of the most difficult to deal with. However, with patience, genuine empathy, self-confidence, and an interest in finding out what is causing the anxiety, wonders can be accomplished.

CAUSES OF STRESS

The upsets people experience, including their manifestation as depression and anxiety, are often caused by unhealthy amounts of stress. The more we know about stress the better we can help others and be able to avoid its unpleasant effects ourselves.

Stress can take many forms and arise in a number of surprising ways, so in some cases stress is hard to identify, its immediate causes difficult to pinpoint. Like depression and anxiety, it can be serious or minor, brief or long lasting, observable and external, or unconscious and internal in origin. Some stress, like anxiety, is necessary for life, because it enables us to cope with potentially demanding factors which continually confront us.

The basic source of stress is *change*. It can be due to changes in amount, type, or form. For instance, too many assignments on the job, a death in the family, an appointment with someone we want to impress, a move to a new area, can all be sources of stress. Stress can arise from happy events in our lives just as much as from unhappy ones. It's true that the happy events may, in the end, put less pressure on us overall, but the important thing to note is it is change—any change—which is the root of stress.

HANDLING STRESS

To handle stress, and to take advantage of its positive effects, it is important to learn how and when stress affects us. To achieve this goal, we must seek to answer several questions about stress:

How does stress manifest itself?

When does it appear?

How can stress be controlled?

What are some of the ways in which stress can be used to advantage?

Stress manifests itself in a number of ways. It can appear in the form of a headache, cold, or back problems, or a number of other physical symptoms. The way to connect a physical ailment with stress is to trace the events leading up to the time when the problem appeared. The timing of a physical or an emotional problem will provide a clue to the cause of the stress. In looking at how and when stress appears, we can then determine what the initial stress was, how it became exaggerated, what was done to try to keep it in check, and what personality factors or behaviors contributed to the undesirable situation.

Mark recently complained of "feelings of nothingness." When questioned about it, he said it had happened to him out of the blue. "I was really happy, then boom, I started to feel lost and empty." When questioned further he said that he had been caught up for weeks in completing his sophomore projects at college before the onset of summer. He had been looking forward to his vacation and was excited about the prospect of getting away from the school. Now that he was home two days, he felt "sort of lost."

The stress in Mark's case seemed to be tied to a number of things. One was the pace, which had been rapid, and then suddenly slowed. This change was due not only to end-of-year tests, but also to the movement from a university setting to home, where the pace was quite different. The sense of loss of purpose in Mark's case probably could have been avoided or reduced if he had prepared himself for the change by anticipating an initial period of relaxation, planning for activities after being home for awhile, and planning ways to initiate new social constellations to enter into in the home environ.

Jill underwent a stressful experience. She took a job in the mountains for the summer, but found the job less stimulating than she had expected. Moreover, instead of going out at night on dates, she discovered she would be working the late shift as a waitress from 9:30 p.m. until 4:00 a.m. After working these hours for three weeks, several unpleasant things happened. First, she got a bad cold. Then she found herself going out after finishing work with some of the other employees to drink at an all-night pub. Finally, she got in trouble with one of her supervisors by blowing up at one of her co-workers over something trivial. When questioned about the blow-up, she said that the thing which caused the outburst had been bothering her for weeks, until she finally couldn't take it anymore.

In taking a new job, there's a certain amount of stress to be expected. This stress is good, too. Dealing with the new and unexpected can help people learn to cope with other, possibly larger, pressures and difficulties in the future. However, in this case, additional stress put too much pressure on Jill's coping skills as well as on her ability to turn the stress to her advantage. Stress tolerance was also lowered because of the unhealthy physical aspects involved, namely, the lack of sleep and the use of alcohol to help her cope.

Psychologically speaking, Jill was denied her expectations, worked under what she considered pressured conditions, and experienced the growth of a small annoyance into a nagging burden that would eventually produce an outburst and subsequent supervisor censure (and additional pressure). In this case, then, instead of the stress of a new situation being an advantage, it became slightly nightmarish.

Yet even Jill's unfortunate experience can be seen in a positive light. By learning from this situation and going over how she handled it, we can help her appreciate how stress can get out of hand, and the kinds of unproductive means she may be tempted to use when dealing with it.

Stress can also result from having to wear many hats in a world that is fast moving and complex. Today the lines of responsibility and action seem vague and unclear, and it is harder to allot time and attention properly. Aaron, for example, complained that the world seemed to be caving in for him, that he was being pulled in a million directions and was feeling terrible as well. On the job, which was in its seasonal high, the work was demanding, complex, and required a good deal of time when he was at the job site, and a good deal of thought when he was home, supposedly resting. His family felt neglected and was angry that he couldn't spend more time with them. It was coming to the end of the two-month busy period and they had had it, and they told him so. Now, he had gotten a bad cold and was feeling physically exhausted. He expressed the feeling that he was failing in every role—father, husband, provider, employee, supervisor, and as a mature person in control.

In working with Aaron, discussions of how he got into this situation proved quite fruitful in planning for when the same busy time would occur next year. Exploring how he might settle things with his family and distance himself for a short period of time when off the job seemed to deflate the immediate pressures and feelings of loss of control that were plaguing him. In other words, by focusing on the development of the problem and the priorities which could be designed, Aaron felt the power of knowledge and control again. This, in turn, helped him to deal more effectively with those he previously just viewed as part of his problem.

So when interviewing someone who appears under a good deal of stress, we should look at what can be learned from the situation. This can be done by getting enough information to establish:

When the person first started to feel pressured

What could be done to recognize potentially hazardous patterns like this in the future

How one can deal with stress when it first appears to prevent it from getting greater, or to reduce it

What factors in the person (i.e., sleeping patterns, use of drugs, lack of food and exercise) make one more susceptible to stress

What alternatives are open now and in the future to help one

enjoy change that is pleasant and deal with change that
is not

What the possible supports are which can be mustered inter-
nally and in the outer environment to help in the handling
of stress

These are general principles. They become specific and useful
when we apply them to people who come to us for help when
they are under a lot of pressure and can't seem to get out from
under it. As we problem-solve with them, they should be able
to work on developing a better style of handling pressure. The
goal is to make them see what specifically led to their being
unprepared for stress, unable to reduce it, and presently unable
to learn from the mistakes they made.

In doing this, we are helping them recognize the areas in
which they are vulnerable, how they can maximize their own
talents and those of others in combatting stress, and how they
can turn present and past stressful incidents into learning experiences for the future.

Chapter 9

Handling a Crisis

In the mental health field, there are times when we need to act immediately. There's no question of waiting things out. We must do something . . . and quickly! If we don't, a mental health emergency may well turn into a disaster. Other instances which require short-term, active intervention but do not have the momentous urgency of an emergency are termed "mental health crises." In both groups—the mental health emergencies and the mental health crises—there is a special opportunity to provide immediate relief and to prevent possible harm. The style of intervention in these situations differs somewhat from basic counseling principles.

Crisis intervention uses general, broad approaches to deal with an array of problems. In the case of a mental health emergency, though, the method employed is normally tailored to the problem encountered. Though there are a large number of mental health emergencies which could arise in one's life, the ones presented below have a significantly greater chance of being encountered in our daily interactions with others. They include self-injurious behavior (suicide and self-mutilation), drug-related emergencies (overdose and bad trips), bizarre behavior, and victim of assault.

SELF-INJURIOUS BEHAVIOR

Frustration, anger, depression, conflict, helplessness, and despair can sometimes lead to behavior that is physically self-destructive. At one time or another, many of us have thought of "chucking it all," "giving up," or "just ending it all." Others of us may not have entertained such thoughts but have done things which proved to be quite self-injurious in nature.

Although self-injurious behavior (SIB) is by no means alien to the human scene, both non-professionals and mental health personnel alike nevertheless become somewhat unnerved when the possibility of SIB and suicide come into play. The threat of such behavior can raise feelings of anger, fear, inadequacy, or any number of negative emotions in a helper. A professional counselor may feel, "If Mr. X commits suicide it will mean that I have failed; what will people think of me as a counselor? Maybe someone else should handle this case, someone who is better than I." A young correction officer may worry about the potential of suicide in one of the cells at night while he's on duty. He may think, "What if someone hangs up tonight while I'm on duty? It will be my fault. He will have lost his life because I didn't do something right. They'll blame me." In a similar vein, someone confronted by a friend who is talking about suicide may want to run away from the situation. "Oh, no. Jim is talking about ending it all. I wish he didn't bring it up with me. What am I to do?"

A brief but basic understanding of what SIB is about is the first step in learning what we can *do* when confronted by a threat of suicide or self-mutilation. It is sometimes helpful to see SIB on a number of continua or ranges of behaviors. As shown on the accompanying chart, these behaviors include the actual threat or attempt at injury, the amount of warning given, the amount of

BEHAVIOR CONTINUA FOR ASSESSING
SELF-INJURIOUS BEHAVIOR

Thoughts about hurting oneself ──────▶ Actual suicide attempt

No warning ───────────────────▶ Numerous warnings

Impulsive or accidental ─────────────▶ Well planned

Diminished state of consciousness ──────▶ Full awareness
   (under influence of alcohol or drugs)

No desire to manipulate others ────────▶ Designed primarily to
                                     manipulate others

planning involved, the physical condition of the person, and the motivation for the self-injurious behavior.

Self-injurious behavior can include anything from expressing some thoughts about hurting oneself to an actual suicide attempt. When professionals assess the severity of a suicide threat, a number of factors are focused upon. Some of the factors which increase the chances that the person will act on the threat include a previous attempt, a close relative who has attempted or committed suicide, alcohol or drug abuse, and the availability of predetermined means to carry out the threat.

Whatever factors are or are not present, it is essential to emphasize that *every threat or warning to commit suicide must be taken seriously!*

One of the prevalent fallacies about suicide is that when a person is really going to commit it, no warning is given. *This is false.* Some people give plenty of verbal warning ("I've decided to end it all") and also give warning through their actions (they may start giving away all of their personal belongings, for example). Others give no hints. One day they just try it.

In some cases, the tragedy results from an impulsive action or an accident. Some people want to show how bad the situation is, but really didn't want to kill themselves. This might have been the case with the actress Marilyn Monroe. She probably hadn't correctly assessed the impact of the drugs she had taken and couldn't do anything to get help in time—the drugs had quickly incapacitated her.

On the other hand, some attempts at SIB are quite well planned. The person may have thought out in minute detail how and when the attempt will be made. The awareness is there. Fatigue, alcohol, drugs, stress are not present to diminish the person's level of consciousness. The person clearly wants to end it all.

A great deal of variation occurs in the amount of manipulation intended. Some people reach out for help by hurting themselves. From the start there's no intention of killing themselves; even the wounds inflicted are superficial. Their whole point is to draw attention to their difficulties and force the situation so someone will help them. On the other hand, others desire merely to end it all. While some in this group feel their death will "show so and so that I meant business," many could care less about the impact their suicide will have. The act is totally self-oriented.

TAKING ACTION WITH THE SUICIDAL

On rare occasions we may come upon a person with a knife, broken glass, or other weapon who is threatening to kill himself. In emergencies such as these, ones involving panic or a calm deliberation to do personal harm, a number of immediate steps need to be taken.

The first action is a "don't." Namely, don't shy away from the situation. In coming upon a scene that requires immediate action, the worst thing we can do is to shrink from it. We may not do the right thing if we stay, but certainly if we run it probably isn't going to help.

When confronting someone who is threatening to jump, stab himself, or do something self-destructive, the immediate goal is to defuse the situation and get the person talking. By doing this we can possibly find out what the person is upset about and stimulate the individual's will to live.

In showing people we take their threats and complaints seriously, we give them the respect they deserve. The resultant possible increase in their personal dignity may provide them with just the change in attitude they need to reassume their desire to survive. Also, when we interact in a way which makes contact with them be it eye contact, voice contact, or emotional contact, they may find the support they need to try life again.

While staying with them, someone else should be sent for help. The kinds of supportive persons needed usually include someone they know, a familiar professional figure (clergy, doctor), and the police. Although we must be as supportive as possible, we must not overstep our authority, either. Not sending for additional help, or trying to rush a person under extreme stress, can result in an unfortunate accident. Remaining calm, trying to talk to the person, and sending for help while actively listening to them is a balanced, commonsense approach.

Such emergencies are rare. In most cases of threatened self-injury, we are not dealing with people who are in immediate danger. Instead, they are at the point of verbally expressing great depression, anger, frustration, or alienation, and declaring that suicide may be the only way out.

In such instances, the first rule is the same as the one in interviewing and counseling—*listen!* This is not the time for pep talks; it is the time to get people to open up and air their feelings. In setting up a situation which is warm and accepting, and in which the helper shows he or she won't become so fearful as to withdraw, people in distress are given a chance to take the first step toward recovery. Where there's hope, there's a chance. And with belief in a chance and the presence of someone to talk to, improvement can become a very realistic possibility to them.

When helping these people, special emphasis should be placed on the development and utilization of other resources. If the person belongs to an organized religion, encouraging the use of the rabbi, priest, minister, brother, sister, or other religious figure may be appropriate. Also, a referral to a psychotherapist, local community mental health clinic, or counseling center is also helpful. The goal is to put them in touch with someone who is trained to deal with extreme depression.

(In an extreme situation where the person is threatening immi-
nent suicide, the person should be accompanied to the
emergency room of the local hospital.) In doing this though,
we should emphasize that we are still available to listen to them
as well.

DRUG ABUSE EMERGENCIES

Urban general hospital emergency rooms are continually
faced with dealing with drug abusers in crisis. Up to 5 percent
of their admissions are related to this problem. Moreover, given
the increasing problems of the drug scene, the percentage will
probably go up before leveling off.

Part of the problem in handling drug abuse emergencies are
the unknown factors involved. For example, drugs tend to
mask other symptoms. Multiple drug use makes it difficult to
determine the causes of certain reactions. Illegal street drugs
vary in their composition and their potency; heroin can be practically "pure" or be mixed with substances ranging from sugar
to rat poison. Furthermore, individual responses to equal
amounts of drugs under similar conditions can vary dramatically. One person's "high" can be another's overdose; one
user's excitement can be another's "bad trip," even though the
dosage is the same.

Despite the unknowns involved, being aware of a number of
points about certain drugs can help us deal with serious situations and quickly forestall greater problems. If we can act intel-
ligently, we can be helpful and supportive in a difficult situation
until medical or psychological/psychiatric care is obtained.

ALCOHOL ABUSE

Two things make dealing with alcohol abuse a little easier
than dealing with some other kinds of drug abuse. One is that

since the liquor industry is regulated and licensed by the government, the danger of getting impurities or toxic combinations in a bottle of liquor is almost nonexistent. Secondly, since most of us have had contact with people who have had too much to drink, we have less of a tendency to shy away from a person in trouble with alcohol because of a fear of making a mistake.

However, though alcohol is relatively uncontaminated by unknown substances, often we don't know how much a person has had to drink. This problem is compounded by the tendency of many people today to be abusers of multiple drugs. People now drink and take sleeping pills, stimulants, hallucinogens, or other types of drugs at the same time. Furthermore, though we are familiar with alcohol abuse, we may not be aware of some of the more serious complications. These include coma, shock, convulsions, delerium tremens, alcoholic hallucinosis, and combative behavior.

An alcohol-induced coma can lead to shock, in which state the person appears pale and sweaty, the skin is clammy, the pulse weak, and fainting may occur. Shock can lead to subsequent total anesthesia of the brain, naturally a very serious complication. Anesthesia of brain could happen several hours after the overindulgence in alcohol.

Prior to falling into a coma the person may appear drowsy, sick, and depressed. In trying to deal with a person in this condition we may meet with combative behavior. The physical complaints reported can include vision problems (e.g., seeing double) and numbness over a large portion of the body. Pallid skin and crossed eyes are other initial symptoms. Later on, a rapid pulse and dilated pupils may appear.

Convulsions are another complication of alcohol abuse. They require medical attention. Convulsions can be serious for a number of reasons. During the convulsions, the person may choke from a blocked air passage because of swallowing his tongue, or he may fall and hurt himself. The convulsions may also be a sign of more serious pathology which requires medical evaluation. Until medical help can be obtained, immediate first aid is required. If possible persons suffering convulsions should be put on their backs, away from hard furniture, have their clothing loosened, and have a soft rolled object (shirt, large handkerchief) put between their teeth so they don't bite their tongue.

Delirium tremens is a rare complication of the hangover stage, usually lasting two to seven days. This condition *requires medical assistance*. One of the reasons for this is that although there are periods of lucidity, the person is generally not in contact with reality. He may not know where he is or who we are—even the most familiar of persons may be seen in a confused light. Disturbing, possibly frightening, hallucinations and insomnia may accompany and complicate the exhaustion this person experiences. Besides immediate first-aid to prevent injury, hospitalization is required.

Alcoholic hallucinosis is different from delerium tremens in that the person appears fine physically but has periods of hallucination and possible delusions (a systematized false belief, e.g., someone is trying to kill me). This is a rare condition which can last for quite variable periods of time depending upon the person. As one might expect, this complication requires immediate medical assistance.

Combative behavior is another difficulty which we can experience with alcoholics. If the person isn't assaultive and one can avoid getting into an argument, combativeness may not increase to the point of needing assistance. However, certain individuals will require assistance or police intervention to prevent harm to self and others.

Depressive behavior in the alcohol abuser merits close supervision. People under the influence of alcohol may lose the inhibition that's been keeping them in check, and as a result their anger may be expressed outwardly (assault, homicide) or inwardly (self-mutilation, suicide). We must pay close attention to the drunken person who becomes so "blue" that self-harm and other highly negative references to self become the theme of his or her comments. Remaining with someone while they're going through such a period in this state of diminished consciousness may be sufficient to prevent an impulsive, dangerous action.

HALLUCINOGENS AND THE BAD TRIP

Many chemical substances have the power to produce sensory distortions and hallucinations. Included in this group are DMT (dimethyltryptamine), DOM (dimethoxymethylamphetamine), and the more widely known LSD (d-lysergic acid diethylamide). These drugs can produce a wide variety of responses. One person may have a pleasurable experience on one occasion and a bad experience at another time. This can be seen in the narrative of a Swiss chemist named Albert Hofmann, who conducted experiments with LSD in the early 1940s. Hofmann describes his experiments in "Psychotomimetic Agents," in A. Burger, ed., Drugs Affecting the Central Nervous System, vol. 2 [New York: Dekker, 1968]. The first experence he had after taking LSD is as follows:

Last Friday, April 16, 1943, I was forced to stop my work in the laboratory in the middle of the afternoon and to go home, as I was seized by a peculiar restlessness associated with a sensation of mild dizziness. Having reached home, I lay in a dazed condition with my eyes closed (I experienced daylight as disagreeably bright) [and] there surged upon me an uninterrupted stream of fantastic images of extraordinary plasticity and vividness and accompanied by an intense, kaleidoscope like play of colors. This condition gradually passed off after about two hours.

He took a subsequent dose several days later. However, his experiences then were quite different:

As far as I remember, the following were the most outstanding symptoms: vertigo, visual disturbances; the faces of those around me appeared as grotesque, colored masks; marked motor unrest, alternating with paresis; an intermittent heavy feeling in the head, limbs, and the entire body, as if they were filled with metal; cramps in the legs, coldness and loss of feeling in the hands; a metallic taste on the tongue; dry, constricted sensation in the throat; feeling of choking; confusion alternating between clear recognition of my condition, in which state I sometimes observed, in the manner of an independent, neutral observer, that I shouted half insanely or babbled incoherent words. Occasionally I felt as if I were out of my body.

When experiences occur which are very undesirable, as in Hofmann's second experiment with LSD, we call it a "bad trip." Medical treatment for this condition usually involves giving medication to reduce anxiety and induce sleep and having someone provide direct interpersonal support and reassurance while the person is tripping.

In most instances, though, particularly in the case of a trip that is unpleasant but not so frightening to produce extreme actions which are dangerous, personal support is the sole action taken. In such cases, other people will be comforting and supportive and can provide feedback to modify the worrisome experiences. One thing to remember, though, is that the person on a bad trip should not be left alone.

OPIATE OVERDOSE

Overdose of an opiate (e.g., heroin or morphine) is an increasingly common drug abuse emergency. Knowing what to do can be crucial because an overdose can cause vital breathing centers located in the brain stem to be depressed to the point where death can occur.

Intentional suicide by overdosing is more common among addicts than nonaddicts. There are many reasons for this, but two major ones are the overwhelming personal and social problems experienced by the addict and the presence of an easy way out by suicide through an overdose.

Accidental overdosing commonly occurs when an inexperienced user takes too high a dose, when the user is misinformed about the potency of the drugs (in some cases the drug may be almost pure), or when a user foolishly resumes the same dose after a period of abstinence (e.g., after incarceration or detoxification period in a hospital). Sometimes, too, a pusher or dealer will decide to eliminate an addict who is becoming a problem by providing him with a lethal dose.

When encountering someone who has overdosed on an opiate, the important thing to do is to call a physician immediately and try to keep the person awake, since depression of the vital breathing centers is a special danger in this case. Some first-aid manuals also suggest trying to induce vomiting.

Problems may occur in the withdrawal stage as well. Barbiturate users, for example, may experience convulsions, psychotic delirium, agitation, and other dangerous physical signs during withdrawal. In cases such as these, the person must also receive medical assistance immediately.

AMPHETAMINE ABUSE

A final drug problem that has become quite common is amphetamine abuse. Amphetamines, also known as "speed," are used legally for obesity and problems of mild depression. Their illegal use as pep pills is also widespread.

Abusers of amphetamines can suffer from problems ranging from malnutrition to what is referred to as "amphetamine psychosis," in which the person appears to have lost touch with reality, is hallucinating, and may be highly suspicious.

A person experiencing amphetamine psychosis may become quite combative and requires a place where stimulation isn't great, since stimulation may exacerbate the symptoms. Consequently, when someone like this is brought into an emergency room, some professionals recommended removing them from the activity of the main area of the emergency room, which is normally quite noisy and active. Our initial efforts to help the amphetamine abuser may include keeping him in a quiet place, but medical help should be secured as soon as possible.

BIZARRE BEHAVIOR

Many unfounded fears which we learn from others are exacerbated by popular folklore and media exaggerations. Mental illness and the so-called nervous breakdown have been given "bad press" down through the ages. Someone who acted strangely was usually ostracized. Possessed, infected, crazy, berserk, bizarre, psychotic, and witch-like are but some of the labels given to people experiencing emotional and organic (physical) difficulties. With nametags as unappealing as these, and the kinds of things the ignorant have attributed to people under extreme mental duress, it's no wonder that bizarre behavior scares people off. They see bizarre, unusual behavior as being totally alien to themselves; consequently it is seen as threatening.

In fact, though, the kinds of behavior we see as bizarre are essentially exaggerations of our own behavior. The behavior has become so pronounced in a particular way due to adverse conditions that are taxing the disturbed person to the limit.

While the behaviors people exhibit are quite variable, a number of categories can be used to assess a person's style of dealing with the world. They include social appropriateness, thought processes (cognition), contact with reality, affect (mood), and self control. Though there are other categories which can be included, these are ones which sufficiently demonstrate how a person's "normal" behavior may become exaggerated when under great stress.

Social appropriateness is always hard to assess. What is normal in one setting may be viewed as unacceptable behavior in other environs or at other times. When under pressure, people may exhibit a disregard or defiance of social norms. Such actions are not very surprising given that we ourselves will throw norms to the wind on occasions when we are very emotional or under the influence of alcohol. When we're very angry or inebriated, for example, we might yell, while in other circumstances we would speak in a normal or soft voice. We might also have problems thinking in a logical fashion (cognition), we might not be clear about what is happening around us (contact with reality), and we might be very emotional (demonstrating extreme affectual responses) and have difficulty preventing ourselves from giving in to impulses we normally are able to suppress without too much effort.

When people suddenly demonstrate bizarre or embarrassing behavior due to psychological problems, the actions they take are merely more extreme versions of the type of unusual things we do when we are upset or in a state where our inhibitions are lowered (by drugs, alcohol, great anger, etc.). Even though the behavior may seem so exaggerated as to seem beyond our understanding, it still should be possible for us to see it within the context of the total human condition. It is important to take this extra step to consider very unusual (psychotic) behavior in this way, because often we must take action while others shun a friend, relative, or co-worker who seems to "break down" suddenly and act strangely. If we join the others in trying to avoid the situation, the person may actually wind up hurting himself or not getting needed help quickly enough. So if we can get over seeing the person who exhibits bizarre behavior as someone to be avoided, we can take the appropriate steps until a physician can be called to provide medication and referral for possible treatment in an emergency room or crisis center.

When dealing with a person who is feeling and acting very strange it is important to provide a supportive, protective environment. The individual may fear he will act upon his own "evil" (unacceptable) urges, be attacked by imagined enemies, or he seems to be in a state of shock.

Another important goal is to allow the person to express himself. To try to confront the false beliefs or take away the hallucinations through reason can result in further deterioration. Here's an example of supportive dialog with such a person:

"I think I feel like I'm a brick falling from the top of a tall building. Can you understand that?"

"I'd like to; can you tell me more?"

"It's a strange sensation. I'm looking down and seeing a ground that would welcome me. It's exhilarating. I could float, but I'm afraid. I want to fall, but I'm concerned the ground would come up too quickly. Do you know what I mean? Have you ever felt that way?"

"The more you tell me the more I can picture how you feel. I think I can understand a little bit better what you're telling me."

The aim is to be supportive, protective, and a good listener. The unusual behavior is often an outward manifestation of how the person feels inside. The person is defending himself from having to feel worse by expressing certain fears, beliefs, and conflicts. To take them away through confrontation would be to take away the last lines of defense.

Try not to humor the person, but listen attentively and be protective and supportive until further professional help can be obtained. In many cases, people express appreciation later for your staying with them and taking them seriously. Some know they were "out of it," but also feel they couldn't help it. When they feel others support their right to express themselves in an attempt to deal with overburdening problems, it is easier for them to maintain their personal dignity than when people shun them or confront them during their difficult times.

THE ASSAULT VICTIM

The physical and emotional shock that accompanies physical assault can be quite overwhelming. Even when a person is just accosted and forced to lie down while being searched and robbed can be traumatic. The sense of helplessness, fears of being molested or killed, and the shame experienced by many victims makes assault a situation in which the person is often under a good deal of stress *after* it's all over. So although victims may need help for their physical injuries following a physical attack, the brutalization of their psyches must also be taken into account.

Jim is a short, stocky executive in his late twenties. He had worked late one night and was exhausted during his trip home by subway. On getting off at his station and starting up the stairs, he was jumped by two young males hidden in an alcove. They put his hands behind his back, told him not to scream, and pushed him to the floor. They then searched him, took his wallet, pants, shirt, and shoes. He was left lying on the floor in his underpants, with his hands and feet tied by his socks and some cord.

After Jim got up and found help, he was brought to the police station. Upon giving them the information they requested, he was picked up by his older brother. As a result of the questions both his brother and the police asked, he began to feel a good deal of conflict. On the one hand, he wanted to tell the story over and over again. (By doing this, people can begin to come to terms with a terrible experience and the emotions they felt during and immediately following it.) However, Jim felt shame, impotence, and inadequacy as a result of how he "handled the situation." The comments by the police and his brother made him feel more and more foolish, not only because of the way they left him (in his shorts), but also because of the fact he didn't fight back. Both his brother and the police asked repeatedly about whether they had a gun and whether they were bigger than him or not, so Jim began to feel small and cowardly. "Why didn't he do something?" was the question he plagued himself with.

Under the circumstances, both the police and his brother had not taken the time to listen to the story with the goal of pinpointing the feelings he had. Recognizing the shock, fear, and impotence at the time of the attack is important when dealing with an assault victim. It is also helpful to support the notion that reacting in a docile way is understandable.

Actively listening to someone relate an emotion-packed incident is one of the most productive intervention techniques we can use. In the case of an assault victim, we will be able to hear the fears, anxieties, anguish, surprise, and helplessness that is often there. This is essential to improvement of the person's state of mind, because once the inner feelings and concerns are out in the open, they become more manageable.

THE RAPE VICTIM

Rape is an act of violence. The victims of this degrading assault go through emotional trials similar to others who have been physically attacked. However, because of societal ignorance and rigid, misplaced, double standards, the rape victim often undergoes additional stress.

First, the rape victim should be treated with the same warmth afforded any victim and brought for medical attention immediately. As in the case of an assault victim, we should recognize the person may be in a state of shock. The individual may seem dazed or show signs of fear. (Victims of rape and assault are frequently threatened if he or she reports the incident.)

The police, hospital personnel, family, and friends will have immediate reactions and attitudes to the rape victim which will affect the victim's outlook. Since many people still erroneously see rape as a sexual act rather than as a violent assault, the people (i.e., family) who normally provide support for the person may be a hindrance instead. Instead of being supportive, they may inflict the victim with their own rage, guilt, fear, or shame. This is particularly the case when a youth is involved.

On the other hand, people who are educated as to the real nature of rape and can be supportive without sharing their own misconceptions and negative emotions can have quite a positive impact. Professionals such as rape counselors, nurses, physicians, and social workers are also in a position to be of significant value in the hospital setting when the rape victim is

brought in for examination. However, the bulk of the therapeutic work may take place at home, with family and friends.

Whether the person is very demonstrative in their emotions,
or quiet, calm, and seemingly in control, the rape victim will
benefit if we take out the time to:

1. Listen actively.
2. Encourage expression of feelings and thoughts about the
attack, even if it seems hard to talk about it at first.
3. Provide an atmosphere in which the person feels at ease in
crying, screaming, or yelling.
4. Be patient with constant repetition of the events and a
continual rehashing of the horror of it: it is usually helpful for a
person to go over something again and again until they can
come to terms with it.
5. Arrange to stay with the person or have some other family
member or friend remain with them for a day or so.
6. Try to find out how she has dealt with terrible episodes in
the past so we uncover the primary way she can come to terms
with the problem. For example, it may be that after some
unnerving event she helped herself bounce back by taking a few
days off and visiting her family; this might be a way for her to
deal with this emergency.
7. Help provide physical comforts such as a meal, a place to
stay, and possibly some clothes.

In addition to the above, supporting the person through the
hospital process, which is quite necessary, can be of great help,
too. If the hospital staff has access to a rape counseling center or
a crisis center, and the person seems to want to talk with someone further about it, helping the person contact them is also
in order.

If the victim is a child, there are other steps to take. The police
and hospital staff are aware of what they are. Special attention
needs to be paid to the family's reactions since they will be taken
as cues by the child as to how he or she should feel about the

incident. This is the reason that many mental health professionals and rape counselors feel strongly about bringing the family in when working with the victim.

As with any mental health emergency, rape can cause a good deal of hardship for the victim. The way we react and the acceptance we provide can help prevent unnecessary harm as well as increase the chances of improvement.

CRISIS INTERVENTION

Crisis intervention is a treatment approach used by mental health professionals. It differs from more traditional and long term treatments primarily in its focus on *active* involvement with a person with the aim of quickly resolving an immediate problem.

Dr. Gerald Caplan, a renowned community mental health specialist, defines an emotional crisis as "a short period of psychological disequilibrium in a person who confronts a hazardous circumstance that for him constitutes an important problem which he can for the time being neither escape nor solve with his customary problem-solving resources." (Gerald Caplan, *Principles of Preventive Psychiatry* [New York: Basic Books, 1964].)

When a person in crisis comes for help to a community mental health clinic or crisis center, the workers often intervene in a way to get the person quickly back into a position where he or she feels able to effectively problem solve on his or her own again. When individuals in crisis appear, it is usually at a time when they are temporarily overwhelmed by something. They feel helpless, frustrated, and at their wit's end.

Normally they would not seek help, nor would they need it. Up to this point, they have had reasonable success with their methods of coping with the world. Now they are faced with a crisis situation and they see no way out.

The goal of the helping agent in this situation is to become actively involved with such persons so that their resources—and

COMMON LIFE CRISES

Job loss
Serious illness or death in family
Divorce
Drug abuse or alcoholism in family
Change of status (retirement)
Money loss
Menopause
Serious financial problems
Fire
Accident
Change of job
Natural disaster
Problems with the law
Loss of self esteem
Educational difficulties
Loss of major opportunity
Major test failure

resources in their environment—can be mustered together for action. With direct manipulation of those in crisis and attention being focused on the symptoms and signs of the problem (not the deep seated causes), the situation can hopefully be turned around in a brief span of time. Once this is done, it is hoped the person can learn from the occurrence rather than merely see it as a past disaster that nothing good came from.

Understanding the nature of a crisis and how to intervene with others is quite important for all of us. Given the physiological and psychological changes we go through in life, all of us can expect to be taxed to the point of breaking at various points. Whether it be the maturational crisis of middle age, the loss of a loved one or some other unexpected occupational, familial, educational, or medical tragedy, we must deal with it effectively, or else suffer greatly from it for longer than is really necessary.

For instance, if our failure to get a particular position left us bitter about the opportunities of life, this outlook might endanger our motivation and personal growth at later periods in life. Whereas if we—possibly with the aid of others—were able to come to terms and overcome the sad occurrence, it might be turned into a plus for the future. We might, for instance, be pushed to strive harder at the job we did get, so that getting further advancement would be possible.

So in crisis intervention, we seek to help the person we're dealing with gain mastery of the situation and of his or her feelings and attitudes as soon as possible. By doing this, the goal is to minimize the harm and show it was a temporary setback, and that the person is now in control again of his or her destiny. This last point is essential if crisis intervention is to work. Not only is it important that we quickly seek to turn the situation around, but the final step is to pull out once things are on the road to being corrected. To prolong involvement in the person's handling of the problem might result in unnecessary dependence.

DIVORCE—AN ILLUSTRATION OF CRISIS INTERVENTION

In some instances when someone becomes involved in a divorce, the person's employer is called upon to intervene and to help the person get back on his or her feet. With the divorce rate so high now in the United States this crisis is becoming more and more common. The hardship divorce causes for the people involved is usually quite notable.

The disruption to children, lifestyle, and a familiar role within society may distress someone to such an extent that all phases of life, including employment, are affected. This happened to Jane, a successful account executive for an advertising agency. After having worked for the firm for ten months in a key position without any problems, she began coming in late and appeared apathetic on the job. Her boss, Bill, did not say anything because he felt it was a temporary situation which Jane would correct herself. When it went on for well over a week, Bill called

Jane in and found out that Jane's husband had sued for divorce. Bill called her in for three subsequent talks on the problem. Following the first one, Jane began to feel a bit better. After the final two-hour discussion dealing specifically with the divorce issue, Jane's work had improved and she began functioning optimally several weeks subsequent to that.

What did Bill do? Was it some sort of miracle? Did he threaten to fire her? How did she improve so quickly? There was no magic involved. He did not threaten her. And although her performance did return quite quickly to its normally high level, it should be noted she was still upset over the divorce; she was acting efficiently in spite of her current feelings. The reason: she felt more in control of the situation and could see a way out.

The way Bill approached the problem is by following a number of key steps, ones that can be used in any number of crisis situations:

1. Permitting airing of feelings
2. Defining the problem in detail
3. Opening up alternatives
4. Offering active assistance
5. Demonstrating how present evidence of success is a prelude to future positive results.
6. Showing that she is still valuable in his eyes.

Specifically the following was done:

In airing her feelings, Jane poured out her heart to Bill. He wasn't pedantic, coarse, or disinterested. He heard her out. Following her discourse on her feelings and concerns, he said that she was successful as a mother, friend, and employee. He reassured her that this problem was only temporary and that they would meet again tomorrow, if she liked, to further define the problem and plan some specific actions.

In defining the problem in detail, Jane reported that she was specifically concerned about (a) her child because she would need to devote more time to her career since she was now responsible for supporting the family, (b) meeting people socially again as a single person, and (c) handling the home as the sole parent.

In opening up alternatives, Bill suggested a number of ways to handle the child-rearing issue—day care, family, friends. Together they looked through the yellow pages and called a number of day-care facilities. As far as the job, Bill said she could probably switch to fulltime at the firm. If not, he had connections in the field. Bill affirmed she would gain more confidence socially and as the sole head of the home once the other points were taken care of. He reminded her about how successful she was in business and in her handling of most of the chores at home already.

In offering active assistance, Bill helped Jane find a social service agency familiar with divorce issues and got hold of several helpful books on the topic.

In reinforcing her success when she started handling the concerns she had, he pointed to her success in doing it as proof that things would work out. He also accepted her right to still feel upset about things and feel weak—after all, she had been married for eleven years. He also started pulling back by suggesting she continue to talk to the divorce counselor recommended by the social service agency.

Bill showed that Jane was still valuable in his eyes by spending time with her and indicating that he expected her to progress. Seeing that others accept us and believe in us when we are feeling helpless is important to our self-esteem and success in dealing with a problem.

The success Bill had in dealing with Jane was not due only to his following the logical problem-solving steps above. It was also because he was courageous, generous, and balanced in his approach. He didn't pull back when she brought up her problem. Instead, he was generous and supportive. He worked with her to deal with the specifics and helped her muster her own personal resources and to obtain other supports from the community.

After being initially quite active he did not continue to be intrusive. He helped her regain her mastery at work and as an independent person. When she needed support he gave it, but he didn't maintain a helping role with her personal problems longer than necessary. He supported her seeing the professional counselor for the purpose that person was hired. He was there when she needed him for just as long as it was necessary. He maintained a helpful, balanced approach.

Rather than feeling lost and ineffectual, several months following the separation she began to feel renewed strength. She was actually better off for going through the crisis. She advanced in business, saw males in a realistic light (the anger she had for her husband was balanced by the positive feelings she had for males like her boss), and she socialized well. What could have turned into a disruptive, continuous crisis ending in her losing her job, her stature in the community, and her self-esteem, wound up successfully instead.

Chapter **10**

Self-Help and Pop-Psychology Books

Browsing through the section marked "Psychology" in a local bookstore is an experience! The titles seem to jump out at you. Ignoring them is practically impossible, not picking them up is an act of true self control. Here is a sampling of the titles available in this often baffling market:

Pulling Your Own Strings
Looking Out for #1 (by the author of
   Winning Through Intimidation)
Born to Win
Don't Say Yes When You Want to Say No
Power!
*Stop Running Scared! Fear Control Training: The New Way to
   Conquer Fears, Phobias and Anxieties*
How to Be Your Own Marriage Counselor
I Ain't Well—But I Sure Am Better
*The Body Language of Sex, Power and Aggression!
   How to Recognize It and How to Use It*

Dress for Success
The Winner's Notebook
I Can If I Want To

How can these tasty morsels be passed up? No matter how healthy and successful a person is, there has to be a title which touches on some sore spot in life. After all, one is never too old (or successful and happy) to learn . . . right?

The question is, though, what exactly can we learn from the array of pop-psychology books now on the market? Are they really beneficial? Can they be harmful? Should we recommend one to a person under some type of stress? And, considering that millions of self-help books are sold each year, why are they so popular?

THE APPEAL OF POPULAR PSYCHOLOGY BOOKS

Self-help books are published in droves each year. It has grown into a multimillion dollar industry. Popular primers and aids for almost every aspect of our lives are available.

One research study which examined the proliferation of parenting primers (K. Alison Clarke-Stewart, Popular primer for parents, *American Psychologist*, April 1978.) noted that almost all parents today read at least one book in the area, and that a significant proportion read more than five. The report also indicated that the information presented in books is also available in articles in many of our popular magazines. The study went on to note:

No question is too trivial; no issue, too controversial. These experts advise mothers on the dangers presented to children by mistletoe and astroturf, baby bouncers and rectal thermometers, circumcision and Zen macrobiotics; they tell parents how to avoid raising a Patty Hearst and what to do if a boy likes pictures of nudes ("Don't worry as long as they're pictures of girls.").

There seems to be a number of reasons why popularized interpretations of psychological, psychiatric, and social work principals are so widely read. One of them is that there are very specific problems which come up in life which many people want immediate answers for.

We have become a symptom-oriented society that thrives on quick action. If a person gets a headache, then take an aspirin—and be quick about it! If someone sneezes more than three times in the same hour, then a full regimen of allergy shots is in order; let's find out the cause and stamp it out.

In the past, patience was the word of the day. If a child was crying and we didn't know the cause, we waited. Sometimes this passive approach was used to extremes, but generally it worked to our advantage. The problem either disappeared spontaneously (most medical and psychological problems are self-limiting, that is, they heal of their own accord if given time), or the cause became more obvious. In the past if we found our adolescent son reading the magazine *Fun-Loving Nudies*, we might ignore it or talk with him about it. Today, however, we seem to run right out to find a book or popular article on the topic. We seem to question our own ability to handle something properly and instead seek out the so-called experts on the topic.

The insecurity some people have today about their ability to handle problems seems more evident now than before. Possibly one reason for this is our lack of role models. Members of families today are not usually clustered in the same geographical area. The impact of this can be profound. In the past if a problem in raising a child comes up, the parents could turn to their parents or other older relatives for advice, or at least to use them as sounding boards. Often this was sufficient. Today we find it difficult to find others we can turn to and rely on for such advice and support.

Furthermore, there is a widespread conception (misconception?) that expert opinion is required in most areas of our lives if we are to avoid unnecessary errors. Belief in ourselves and in each other is being replaced by reliance on designated professional others.

This is another example of the pendulum swinging too far in the other direction. In the past our total dependence on common sense, which contained many useless and harmless myths, sometimes got us into trouble. For instance, a once believed cure for most ills was food, drink and rest. We now know that if a person hits his head and might have a concussion, the worst thing you can do is feed him and put him right to bed. There is a limit to unexamined common sense.

Medical, psychological, and other scientific communities have taught us much. However, these teachings are not meant to replace our own initiative and knowledge about life, but rather to complement it.

Another possible reason for our high interest in pop-psychology books is the great level of frustration we face in modern life. TV, radio, and the printed media spew out the opportunities and advantages of luxurious living. Many, however, find it hard to realize the goals and possess the good life that we see being projected. Thus, the frustration grows and we look for a way out. We buy lottery tickets, subscribe to periodicals about money, and purchase books on how to make a million dollars in twelve easy lessons.

"The feeling of disillusionment about life is heard in many different quarters:

"I've worked for years on my Ph.D. in history and I can't get a job."

"I'm killing myself in the respected profession of nursing and they pay me less than a student working in a supermarket."

"I've been good, haven't landed in jail, and the only job they offer me is dishwasher at a salary equal to what I would make by selling dope for five minutes on the corner of the street where I live."

The economically well off are often just as disillusioned. They see the good life painted as having a key position, money, two cars, a house, and 1½ dogs—and yet they're still not happy. It's quite confusing since they were told this would cure all emotional ills. Where do they turn? Naturally, to the book, *Rich and Depressed: How to Cure it*.

And so it's no wonder why the self-help and pop-psychology market is so great today. There is a ready demand for authoritative, quick-cure books. The question remains, though: Are there problems in using these types of books which we should know about?

THEIR LIMITATIONS

One of the key problems in obtaining a personally useful self-help book comes at the very beginning in the selection of it. We want to know which book is right for us and the problem we're faced with now.

Many books promise so much. They try to deliver information or "their message" to a wide audience. There seems to be a basic assumption that the solution, like a one-size garment, fits all. This is naturally not the case. Economic, socio-cultural, ethnic, race and other differences seem to be ignored or seen as irrelevant. It's left up to the reader to apply the message to their own situation.

Another difficulty in selecting the right book for your problem is that your problem may not be what it appears to be. For instance, a shy person may seek a book on being assertive because it seems to be the most suitable for the problem. However, the problem may lie with self-esteem; possibly a book on liking yourself as a calm, quiet and strong person is what is needed. (Trying to be like the other guy, rather than happily being more at home with your style of dealing with the world, is not always the best answer.)

Similarly, mistakenly avoiding a book which might be helpful is also possible. An aggressive, hostile woman may avoid a book on projecting herself because she feels she is outgoing enough, when in fact if the book were a good one it would demonstrate that what she sees as being assertive is actually destructive aggression. If she knew which book to read, she might actually benefit from the message it held.

This brings us to another major difficulty with these types of improvement books, namely that many of them require a personal guru to implement the message given. People read them and either say "What then?" or somehow try to apply the technique in a haphazard and possibly harmful way.

If the book is designed to be part of a course it should say it. If it has the shortcoming of only opening up an area which requires some practice and further reading before being of some help, it should note it in black and white.

Some of those books which seem to need a teacher delivered with it are confusing because the approach expounded is too idiosyncratic for it to be applied easily and effectively in an array of situations. This is often hard for the reader to see, and it can be very frustrating because of the manner in which the solution is given.

For example, often a book on some aspect of assertiveness (e.g., being a leader in business, speaking out with confidence in a group setting) is written by a charismatic person who has a flare in presenting a philosophy that sounds attractive, but which does not take into account the particular difficulties of the readers. In addition, while it is inspirational, few concrete steps are given to help the person test out the theory and methods which are being proposed.

We all accept the tenet that what works for one person may not work for another. However, the attractive way in which some methods are presented makes one think that you'd have to be an imbecile or loser not to be able to follow the golden arrows to the success tree. This appeal is not very surprising considering the fact that some self-help books are put together by writers whose primary expertise is in creating an attractive package. Even in the case where "experts" are used, the message is often so boiled down and popularized that it is lost in the process.

In scientific publications, each point needs to be documented and supported by research findings, but those writing for a general audience have a much greater latitude. This sometimes poses a problem, part of which can be dropped in academia's lap. By trying to stick only to the facts and provens, those involved in fruitful research have provided almost no forum for exchanging creative hypotheses. Newsstand magazines are left to popularize certain ideas, but their readers do not have ready access to a body of knowledge concerning the subject which might indicate that the ideas being expanded are not supportable. Mental health professionals, however, would readily recognize where the facts were replaced by proselyting or hypothesizing.

Another factor in assessing the worth of today's self-help publications is that what appears in a mass circulation magazine or in paperback as a new idea may be in fact an exaggeration of one part of an accepted theory in social work, psychology, or psychiatry. A publically acclaimed therapeutic breakthrough may in actuality be a distortion or a caricature of some approach commonly used in psychotherapy today. If the "new idea" were presented to professionals, this would (hopefully) be quickly recognized. The average layman might not see the "new" theory for what it is: a not-so-new twist on an old technique. To see several different books touted as innovative when they actually say the same thing, the only difference being that the messages are rehashed in other terms and given new costumes, can also be very disheartening to the person looking for help.

A number of books, in an effort to capture the audience, almost sensationalize basic concepts in the process. The frequently meaningless jargon used by mental health professionals is bad enough, but anger or anxiety caricatured or simplistically overdrawn *so the public can understand the concepts* can be equally disconcerting—and can have deleterious affects.

For instance, being expressive of how one feels is a ground rule in most psychotherapies. The therapist wants the person to open up so together they can look at what the person is thinking and feeling about an issue. This opening up can have many beneficial effects, one of which is that the person learns not to bottle up all his or her emotions. In some self-help books, though, this point is exaggerated and people are told to tell everyone just how they feel at that moment. This leads to unfortunate results because it doesn't take into account the temperance called for in interpersonal relations. In psychotherapy, tact and charity in our relationships are not voided, they are put into perspective. In some books, however, this doesn't happen; consequently, aggressiveness rather than appropriate assertiveness is taught, which results in problems for the unaware reader.

Probably the most serious problem resulting from the improper use of self-help books is the letdown felt after the temporary high of reading a self-help book or applying a pop-psychology message. The degree of the letdown is naturally quite variable. The phenomenon is similar, though, to the problems a number of professionals had to deal with as a result of the proliferation of sensitivity groups some years ago. People would enter what was termed a "growth institute" where they would take part in marathon groups with untrained or poorly trained leaders. The emotions would run high; the promises made would be great; many would leave with lofty goals, their weaknesses laid bare, their resolution firm . . . for the moment anyway.

When the group disbanded, the disillusionment would start to set in. They would not remember or be able to retain the glow of excitement and group solidarity. They would recall quite vividly how their faults had been put in the limelight. They would remember how their defenses had been broken down and fingers had been pointed at them.

This disillusionment, combined with the lack of support which was previously present, ended for some in great hardship. They were confused, disheartened, quite upset, and burnt out. Some sought out professional therapy to work the issues out. Others remained disillusioned and upset about the onslaught on their sensitivities they had subjected themselves to.

With self-help books, a mild form of disillusionment and

discomfort is possible. People read the message, totally absorb the charismatic presentation, and become convinced they have found *the* answer. Since the immature part of us naturally seeks the easy way out (the "golden key"), it's no wonder that people want to find *the* answer to their depression, anxiety, or other pressing problem with a minimum of delay and effort.

The answer to a problem is often not an easy one. Problems usually don't grow up overnight. The solutions, likewise, will not appear in the short span of a few hours. So to get involved in a book or philosophy and swiftly get a high from it may be initially most pleasant, but the trip back down can be disturbing.

With so many cautions on the limitations of selecting and employing self-help books, one might wonder whether a pop-psychology book can be of any value. Despite the many drawbacks and problems with a number of them, the answer is still yes.

THEIR ADVANTAGES

If chosen and employed correctly, certain popular books in the mental health area can prove valuable. In some cases, they can provide examples of how others dealt with a problem. This may be all we need to break the stalemate we feel in confronting the issue at hand. Or we may just need the assurance that our thoughts on something are not too far out. By hearing an "expert" agree with us we may be able to muster the courage to move ahead. Also, knowing other people have lived through and overcome their difficulties can be a much-needed inspiration to continue trying in the face of grief, anxiety, or other problems. So motivation-building and supportive data are two positive things we can get from some self-help books.

Some books may offer us an insight into different perspectives on dealing with an issue. If the authors don't present it as the be all end all, and we appreciate their views as one approach rather than *the* most effective method, it can be quite helpful. In such instances the different view of life can be all we need to help us get through a particular problem. The book is not bringing necessarily new concepts to bear, but putting what we know in a more useful sequence; and it is in this light that the book should be employed.

For instance, several years ago I was sitting on my back terrace trying to decide how to begin a talk I was scheduled to give on adolescence. The point I wanted to key in on was turmoil, but I wasn't clear how to approach it. Just then I was distracted by my new neighbor who had started tearing up a corner of his yard where the previous owner had put down green cement blocks to cover the ground. I went over to him to pass the time of day (and to find out what the heck he was doing).

I asked him if he was going to dig out the grass that grew up every year between the blocks. The grass between the blocks drove my former neighbor wild. No sooner would he pull them out, when they would pop up again, and it seemed no weed killer could control them. My neighbor said he had a different plan. Instead of trying to constantly control the grass, he had decided to remove the green cement blocks and try to cultivate the grass so it would grow properly. He felt it would take more effort to fight the grass and that it would look better if it were permitted to grow more fully.

Now I knew I had the idea I needed for talking about the turmoil in adolescence. It had always been a problem for me to explain how parents might deal with rebellious children. Possibly if I encouraged patience, and told this story, they would be willing to share the new insight I had. Namely, that what appears like rebelliousness, ("that damned grass") may actually be beautiful youthful strength trying to exert itself (and grow). Rather than clamping down on *every* independent or "aggressive" action, we should try to encourage new initiatives within reasonable limits. Just as the neighbors' actions helped me see things in a different light, some self-help books can do the same.

Some books are also valuable in teaching problem-solving techniques. Rather than trying to impose values on us, they help us organize our own beliefs and resources so we can tackle problems which previously seemed beyond our capabilities. This can be especially helpful when all we need is to implement proven, well-researched techniques to achieve our goal and maximize our talents.

Probably the most valuable popular mental health books are those which provide factual, detailed information, in an honest, sophisticated fashion. There are some excellent books on human sexuality, hyperactivity, stress, and other socio-psycho medical topics. For example, if we are looking for a book to tell us about psychotherapy, we can now get a balanced book on the subject which gives us the pros and cons on the total process and looks at the complex issues involved in entering therapy. An informative book on a topic we are interested in may also permit us to make decisions which we couldn't before due to our lack of data and confidence.

There's no reason why all of us shouldn't have access to the findings of medicine, psychology, and other professions. This becomes possible when good writers help mental health professionals prepare their material in a way that it becomes more practical and understandable to the general audience. Yet this is not easy, and some writers and professionals do not present their material in a responsible fashion. This detracts from the efforts of good writers and professionals who can present their findings in a readable fashion. This is most unfortunate, since it is important that the public be informed of advances in the sciences and arts.

SELECTING, USING, AND RECOMMENDING THEM

A self-help book for personal use or for use by someone else who seems to need help should be practical, factual, detailed, specific, and viewed in the limited perspective for which they were designed. Some recommended guidelines in selecting a self-help book are described in the paragraphs below.

1. Be a critical consumer of self-help books: carefully evaluate

your need and the products which seem to meet it in advance of purchase.

2. Determine the kind of information you need by reflecting on the problem at hand, how it has been approached thus far, what other people think the problem is, and what information you already have at your fingertips.

3. Before buying a book on some topic, preview it. Skim through it in the bookstore, evaluating the topics covered in the table of contents and index, or borrow the book first through the library.

4. Set your goals in line with the type of book you're buying or borrowing. If you're looking for something to inspire or motivate, don't look for an in-depth book on some aspect of mental health. Don't expect the book to provide a continual uplift—then you won't run the risk of being let down.

5. Be critical of the book and the author. It doesn't matter if they have letters or affiliations after their names. (Professors make mistakes, too!) The authors couldn't possibly know your circumstance, and just because they're right in some instances, doesn't mean you are necessarily wrong. You'll get more out of what you read in psychology and psychiatry if you understand that these professions are arts as well as sciences.

6. If you're looking for an authoritive volume on some topic, look to see if there are references so you can read further on a topic. If you know someone in the field, you might find it useful to ask them about the findings presented. Reviews by respected professionals are also usually available.

7. Recognize that no matter how good a book is, it can't take the place of getting information from someone who knows you or the person needing help and the problem that is being confronted.

The last point is essential. No book can take the place of contact with another caring human being. Nor can the information contained in an in-depth text replace a course on the topic or a thorough discussion with a person familiar with the

area. This is the philosophy of *Helping Others*. While the information in this volume can help you extend your natural talents,
it cannot make you a professional counselor, be as good as a
course on the topic, or present material in detail as do the books
listed in the bibliography . . . nor is it intended to be or do any
of these things!

Recommending self-help books should be considered when
working with others (particularly books on problems such as
stress, where the information can be helpful as an adjunct to the
person's problem-solving process). But self-help books should
never be used to replace the help we, as friends, family, or
acquaintances, can give by our personally reaching out to the
person in need. As a matter of fact, if more people took an
interest in helping others, pop-psychology books of questionable value would probably not empty as many pocketbooks, no
matter how tempting the titles were.

Chapter 11

Obtaining Professional Help

Part of knowing how to help someone is knowing when our efforts will *not* be enough. In standing by another person in distress, there are times when through our support, active listening, and assistance in the problem-solving process we come to believe that a special, professional consultant might be useful. Once this seems evident it should be brought to the person's attention and discussed. Then, if the person comes to see that seeking additional assistance is best, helping him or her find professional aid may be necessary. Recognizing that one needs additional assistance and that there are many options open when seeking it is difficult for many people. Therefore, having a basic knowledge in this area can be most useful for those of us interested in helping others.

DETERMINING THE NEED

When does a person need professional help for an emotional problem? There's no pat answer for this. It obviously depends upon the person and the problem. Probably one of the best ways to arrive at a decision is to assess the person's behavior and reported symptoms in terms of the following questions:

How exaggerated or severe is the behavior or problem being experienced?

Is the problem or the symptoms very unusual or bizarre in nature?

Is the person quite baffled as to the cause or solution to the problem?

How much is the difficulty interfering with the person's overall functioning?

Does the behavior seem to be getting worse?

What has the person already tried in an effort to deal with the problem?

How severe is the problem? A recent study reported that surgery has often been recommended and conducted when it was unnecessary. In such instances the trauma to the body and the financial costs incurred could have been avoided. The same can be said of psychotherapy, professional counseling, and drug therapy. Psychotherapy and other professional mental health treatments are frequently sought and recommended when their need is simply not indicated. People seek it when they shouldn't because of their being misinformed, too dependent, or because they see it as being a chic thing to be involved in. Some therapists encourage people to go into treatment when they shouldn't because of inexperience, a poor understanding of the limitations and uses of therapy, and plain old greed.

Consequently, prior to making a decision to seek out or recommend a professional for a consultation, it is wise to look at the problem and the other resources open. In doing so the chances are increased that unnecessary cost, time, and emotional investment can be avoided.

The severity of a problem is one of the keys to knowing whether professional assistance should be sought. Feeling a bit down, anxious, or confused is not cause for alarm in itself. Only when the situation becomes extreme should outside help be given consideration.

A good example of this is the grief reaction. If someone close dies, a person naturally becomes somewhat depressed. This could last for some time, ranging from weeks to possibly months. As a matter of fact, the person, particularly a spouse of thirty or so years, may have short periods of the blues for the rest of his or her life. This is not a cause for undue concern.

However, if the person is severly depressed for month after month, begins developing a number of physical ailments, and doesn't seem to adjust at all, the situation may possibly be abnormal. The key is the *severity* and *duration* of the reported symptoms and observable signs. If a reaction is out of proportion with the cause in terms of magnitude or persistance, then it is usually wise to seek outside help to be on the safe side.

The outside help may initially be seeing a physician who can temporarily precribe a psychotropic drug (one designed to affect behavior or mood), or going to a member of the clergy for support. From that point on, if the problem still persists, then further referral to a psychotherapist may be indicated.

Some examples of the types of situations which might point to the need for a professional mental health evaluation include:

Persistent, severe depression

Overwhelming anxiety

Frequent loss of self control (e.g., frequent anger verbally or physically demonstrated without an ability to prevent its expression)

Incapacitating guilt

Extreme hesitancy in dealing with daily problems

Continuous preoccupation with personal health

Great irrational fears (phobias)

Persistent marital difficulties

Spiraling family problems

Inability to adjust to change

Excessive drinking, gambling, use of prescribed or illegal drugs

Chronic sleeping or eating problems

Inability to develop good interpersonal relations

Difficulty in holding a job

Serious school problems

Extreme dependency reflected in an inordinate fear of independent, adult-like behavior

Great difficulty in relaxing

Little ability to concentrate

Compelling desire to please others—and the fear of not being
able to do so

Are the symptoms bizarre?   A professor was once asked by
beginning psychology students how one could distinguish between normal and neurotic behavior.   While admitting it was
very difficult and the line between normal and neurotic was not
often distinct, he offered the following basic explanation: So-
called normal people get upset, have conflicts, and occasionally
get anxious.   Sometimes when they are anxious or under stress
they use coping mechanisms such as suppression (consciously
trying to put something out of one's mind) and unconscious
mechanisms such as rationalization (excuse making), so they
won't have to feel the impact of the bad feelings caused by
what's happening.   Neurotic people, on the other hand, use
defense mechanisms to such an *exaggerated* degree that two
things happen: (1) people begin to notice they are strange, and
(2) the use of their defenses is so great that it interferes with the
execution of their daily activities.

Even given this basic differentiation between "normal" and
"neurotic" behavior, there is great difficulty in determining
what behavior is actually deviant.   What may appear to be
bizarre in one culture is quite acceptable in another.   What may
be unusual for one person is the norm for another.

Yet a number of behaviors are *generally* termed as unusual,
and merit follow-up.   In most of these cases, the persons themselves question their feelings and behaviors.   In the instances
when they don't, the helper can bring them to their attention to
see their reaction and the explanation given for them.

Some of the more predominant bizarre behaviors or experiences that people most often report are:

Seeing, hearing, or smelling things that are not present in reality (hallucinations)

Having systematized false beliefs (delusions), for example, that people are plotting against them, that they have special powers, or that people are watching them or talking about them

Having strange ideas or thoughts which can't be controlled by telling yourself they are illogical

Having unusual urges or compulsions to do things which are recognized to be strange or silly

Sometimes losing contact with reality; not being able to tell whether something is fantasy or real

Is the person baffled by the problem's cause or solution? "I just can't figure out what's causing me to feel this way. I've tried everything; I can't seem to get a handle on the situation." Complaints like these are not uncommon, because some people are extremely perplexed by the difficulties they face. The problem may not necessarily be a big one, but the cause of it or their efforts to handle it appropriately seem to have reached a dead end. In cases such as these, a friend or associate can often be of help. However, there are other times when no amount of help seems to have significant positive results—then the need for professional mental health techniques arises.

People with pervasive depression and free-floating anxiety, which seems not to be associated with a particular cause, often require professional help. The problem has undoubtedly developed over a long time, and short-term treatment by a nonprofessional will probably prove ineffective. Moreover, with a problem that is vague and amorphous, it is easy for a friend or acquaintance to get frustrated and upset in handling it. There is seemingly no end or improvement in sight, and in such instances it is natural to get angry or oppressed by the situation.

When the cause seems quite evident but the solution seems elusive, problem-solving efforts with a professional might also be required. Sometimes an educated, warm, accepting family member or friend can help, but there are occasions when such efforts prove fruitless though. In these cases, an evaluation by a specialist would be in order.

How much is the problem interfering with daily activities? Some problems seriously affect the person on a daily basis. If the person's anger is such that he or she is losing jobs and friends left and right, then something has to be done. If the person is so nervous all the time that even minimal risk-taking is short-circuited and adulthood is smothered by a constant need to be dependent upon others, then seeking professional support and intervention seems warranted.

Some people respond to difficulties by allowing their world to become more and more constricted. Although withdrawing from active interpersonal pursuits may temporarily alleviate the pressure brought on by interacting with others, it is also a nonproductive way out of the anxiety. The more one withdraws, the more one loses the benefits of our social occupational, and personal environments. People are social beings. By withdrawing from social contacts, we are putting ourselves in an abnormal situation.

Another problem in withdrawing from social contacts is that we increase our future vulnerability. The more we are in touch with people, the more we recognize their foibles, shortcomings, beauty, and humanness. If we put ourselves in a corner, our ideas become more and more unrealistic regarding others.

Narcotic addicts often blame people in their environment (pushers, addicted friends, unsupportive parents) for their problems. Some get so angry and vindictive that during their initial rehabilitation period they note their conviction not to "bother with anybody" upon release. In working with them, one of the goals is to show them that it is important to be discriminating in who they spend their time with. However, cutting themselves off from everyone until they find the one person they can trust may be frustrating and disillusioning because once they get fed up with being alone, they might reach out in desperation, be disappointed in an inadequate response, and return to the shell.

Withdrawing from an environment which is anxiety producing can be a Catch-22 situation in the making. The more a person withdraws, the more sensitive he or she becomes to the comments and harmless barbs of others, and this leads to further withdrawal. Some avoidance of our problems is understandable, but when avoidance becomes so pervasive that it interferes with our daily activities, a mental health evaluation is indicated.

Does the behavior seem to be getting worse? With the exception of rare mental health emergencies or crises, most of the problems which debilitate people are quite insidious in nature. They develop by such imperceptible degrees that the upset or anxious individual may not even recognize that the problem has gotten out of hand. In interviewing someone, therefore, we always look for the baseline. When did the problem start? How bad was it then? What is the impact of it now? Through questions like these the comparison can be brought out into the open so both the helper and the person needing counseling can see the status of the difficulty.

If the person has gotten to the point where he or she feels overwhelmed by the problem even after seeking help from friends, relatives, and community supports such as the family physician, then further professional help from a mental health specialist would seem warranted.

What has the person already done to deal with the problem? This question refers specifically to whether the person has already tapped other resources in the community to help with the problem. In other words, have they already talked with their physician, religious leader, or other significant person who might normally fill an informal family counseling role?

Utilizing these resources is an important step because it may make additional assistance unnecessary. Many members of the clergy have counseling experience and training and can intervene to shortcircuit a problem before it gets worse. Physicians can sometimes provide the reassurance and temporary medication to get a person through a crisis so it does not become a prolonged problem. Also, the physician and other influential

professionals with whom the person has contact can often recommend a psychologist, social worker, family counselor, or
psychiatrist with whom they have had positive contact. So,
finding out who the person has already approached is important
before talking with them about going to a therapist.

HOW TO SUGGEST PROFESSIONAL HELP

Recognizing that someone appears to need professional help
is only the first step. Telling them they may need it can be an
ordeal itself because of the stigma attached to seeking help in the
area of emotional or mental health.

Being in therapy can be viewed in very negative or very
desirable terms. Some feel that psychotherapy is very chic—
particularly if the therapist has the right address, high fees, and
a known reputation. For a period of time, and still in some
circles, being in analysis with certain professionals was the
"in thing."

On the other end of the spectrum, therapy can be viewed as a
real stigma. This is especially the case for some families who
view therapy as proof that the person can't work it out on their
own and are weak. They never think that the reason the person
may be in therapy is to further actualize certain capabilities and
strengths which are temporarily stymied.

The family may also object because they see the need for
therapy as proof of their own failure. Instead of encouraging a
troubled or upset son or daughter to seek outside support, they
fight it because they believe if the child goes it will mean they
were failures as parents.

Even the "liberal" segment of our society in many instances
harbors mixed feelings about therapy. They may recommend it
for others, but if they need it themselves, it's like pulling teeth to
get them into it. One therapist trainee who used to come for
supervision to the office in which I did therapy used to make it a
point to try to look like a doctor (whatever a "doctor" is supposed to look like) when visiting my office. One day when he

was stopped by the new doorman at my building. The doorman asked where he was going. When he said he was coming up to see me, the doorman said he was sorry he had stopped him, but he didn't know he was a patient of mine. At this the intern became flustered and started to explain that in fact he wasn't (just) a patient, but actually a doctor.

Dealing with the blocks a person might have against going into therapy is usually necessary when bringing up the topic with someone. There's no way to get around these potential difficulties, and no need to try.

A number of things to keep in mind when recommending outside help for someone are as follows:

1. Be clear and direct about why you think they should consider asking an expert about the problems they're facing.

2. Be clear in your mind about what you want to say before bringing the topic up. Have your own feelings about therapy clear in your mind, too, and be aware, *prior* to bringing the topic up, of the potential responses you may receive. This will reduce the chance that you will seem self-conscious about discussing it and the chance that the other person will feel uncomfortable as a result of your own uneasiness.

3. Bring the topic up in a private area. This is a serious and personal issue, and it should be given the privacy and attention it deserves. If the person responds by joking, don't jump in and fool around as well. Some people laugh when they're nervous. You don't want to convey the feeling that you think the problem of emotional distress is a funny or unusual one.

4. If pressed about the repugnance of going to a "shrink," the role of a clinical social worker, psychiatrist, or psychologist should be put in the perspective of a specialist in interpersonal relations and mental health. They probably wouldn't hesitate to go to a medical specialist or a lawyer, so why should they balk at going to another type of specialist who can possibly facilitate their handling of an issue? One definition of therapy is that it is an intensified form of the normal process of growth.

5. Reading can be encouraged on the topic. There are a

number of books out on this subject which can be quite helpful. Several of them are described in the bibliography at the end of the book.

In conducting the discussion in the above manner, while leaving ample room for the person to react and ask questions, the topic of therapy can usually be broached in a very beneficial fashion, with a minimum amount of discomfort for both the helper and the person being helped.

When discussing obtaining professional assistance, it is very important to help the person develop a proper consumer's attitude. Mental health therapies such as psychotherapy, drug therapy, and behavior therapy represent a service, not a magical ceremony. The more a person knows about the services available and what they entail, the better off he or she will be. Reading one or more books recommended on obtaining help can be of immense help. Some people will not read them though, but those who do will benefit from the practical information on the topic.

In trying to inform the person of the nature of therapy, we should try to provide at least some material on the following areas:

What to expect when going for a mental health evaluation

What settings one can go to for help

The different professions offering mental health assistance and how to find a therapist

The major types of therapies

The general fee range, possible insurance reimbursement, and commitment expected when in therapy

The rights one has as a person in therapy

Given the broad range of issues the person may be concerned about in going for help, other questions and areas may be touched upon. However, the topics listed above will deal with most of the questions people present.

THE MENTAL HEALTH EVALUATION

What should be expected when going for a mental health evaluation? The particular style of the evaluation may differ from setting to setting and therapist to therapist, but there are a number of common characteristics which can be described. For example, most professionals will spend one to three sessions eliciting information. Some may also employ psychological testing if the interviews do not seem to provide them with enough data to make an initial assessment. By the end of the evaluation period, enough information should be out in the open for feedback to be given to the person as to what kind of treatment, if any, is needed. If professional assistance is required, and the person wishes to enter counseling or some type of therapy, then the ground rules should be set. Essentially, such information is given along with an agreement on the therapeutic goals.

Deciding on therapeutic goals is quite essential since it will provide the framework for subsequent sessions. These goals will usually be set according to the person's responses to the following questions:

What problem brings you in?

How long has this difficulty been bothering you?

What made you come in now for treatment?

How have you tried to handle this difficulty in the past?

What do you think is causing it?

What kinds of problems has this difficulty been causing you in life?

Are there times when the problem seems to be worse?

What do you think professional treatment can do for you?

What are some other, possibly related, issues you want to work on?

What are the assets and limitations you feel you have in dealing with these problems?

In an evaluation, then, the person is expected to provide

details about the complaint, what has been done about it, how it is impacting on the person's overall functioning, and what the person's expectations are for professional treatment. Based on the answers to these questions, and possibly on some information about the person's past and present interpersonal environment, the professional will give her or his opinion about treatment. With this opinion out in the open, goals can be formulated and the ground rules of therapy be set out clearly, so each participant knows his or her responsibilities.

GROUND RULES OF THERAPY

Before making a verbal contract to enter into any treatment, the following information should be obtained by the client or patient:

When will the treatment begin?

How long will each session last?

How often will the sessions be?

What will the cost be for each session?

What will the arrangements be for payment?

What if a session has to be missed?

What will the person be expected to do in treatment?

How long will the treatment go on?

Finding out when treatment can begin is important because many clinics and practitioners are quite backlogged with an on-going caseload. Consequently, though the intake evaluation may be done almost immediately after calling for an appointment, treatment may be postponed for weeks or months.

Sessions usually last between thirty minutes and an hour, and can occur from one to five times per week. On the average, unless the treatment of choice is psychoanalysis, the person usually is asked to come in one or two times per week for their sessions.

The cost for therapy or professional counseling varies a good deal, depending on whether the treatment is done in a clinic or privately. The range in clinics is $5 to $30. Private treatment is considerably higher: $20 to $100 per session. The average cost per treatment also varies according to geography. In many areas of Connecticut the sessions are $70, in New York, $50 to $60, and in Philadelphia, $40 to $50. These fee ranges are naturally subject to change, depending upon the economy, the law of supply and demand, and so on.

The arrangements for payment should also be discussed. Some therapists require payment after every session; others will permit the patient to pay either at the end of the month or at the end of each session. The client's insurance is also a factor. Most private therapists require payment for services and leave it to the patient to get reimbursement, if possible, from his or her health insurance company. Most clinics, and a minority of therapists, however, are willing to take part of the fee and wait to be reimbursed by the insurance company. This arrangement is more frequently made when the patient is having problems in meeting the medical bills because of a low income.

If a session is missed, there is almost always a general rule that twenty-four hours prior notice must be given or else the patient must pay for the session. One reason for this is that the therapist reserves the patient's time on the same day each week, and filling it on a moment's notice is next to impossible. Another reason is to discourage patient's cancelling whenever he or she doesn't feel like going. When a person doesn't feel like going, it is probably one of the best times to go so the feelings can be discussed openly with the therapist. In therapy, unlike in surgery or dentistry, the relationship with the professional is the most important part of the treatment, not just a secondary factor.

What the person will be expected to do in therapy should also be discussed. It will vary from therapy to therapy, but it is imperative that the person be clear as to what his or her role will be and the responsibilities he or she will have. This will avoid uncertainty and unnecessary anxiety.

The length of the treatment is also an important issue. In certain brief problem-solving therapies the duration of treatment may only be five to ten sessions. However, other therapies usually require the person to come for a longer period. Though the therapist may not know exactly how long it will take to work through the problems presented, by getting at least an idea of expected duration, the person will not be caught off-guard and feel they have been drawn into a longterm situation they didn't want or anticipate.

TYPES OF MENTAL HEALTH WORKERS

"Where should I go for help?" is the next question usually asked by people once they decide to reach out for professional help. The choices in most areas, particularly urban ones, are usually wide. Most areas today have community mental health centers. These public clinics, and the private psychiatric/social service agencies, provide help to thousands of people each year. The names of local clinics and agencies can be gotten from your church or synagogue, your physician, the United Fund Agency, a local mental health association, an area medical college, or by looking in the yellow and white pages of your phone book. Probably the best way to locate a clinic or therapist is through some person you know in the helping professions (medicine, psychology, psychiatry, social work, religion, law, or fraternal organization).

When selecting a service, be aware that most clinics today are interdisciplinary, so you may receive help from someone specializing in any one of several helping professions. Similarly, when seeking assistance on a private basis, there are a number of types of professionals to choose from. The three traditional mental health professions—social work, psychology, and psychiatry—are prevalent in both private and clinic settings. In addition, there are certified family therapists, marriage counselors, and other specialists with a variety of training.

Social workers in clinical practice generally have both a four-year college degree and a master's degree in social work (MSW or MSS). In addition to academic work in understanding and treating emotional problems, the social worker has received supervised experience in working with people with problems. While some social workers doing therapy have less or more education in the area, certification and licensing for clinical practice by most states comes after they have received their master's degree and give evidence of a number of years of supervised post-master's work.

A number of registries of qualified health care providers in social work are published. Also, the Academy of Certified Social Workers offers a certifying examination to those who meet their minimum qualifications; those who pass can put the letters ACSW after their name.

Psychologists usually possess a doctorate degree (Ph.D., Psy.D., Ed.D.). To be licensed they must also pass an examination and show proof of supervised experience. Not all psychologists are licensed to do clinical work; instead their primary interests may be research or teaching. Clinical psychologists, however, have had supervised work with people in distress. Like social work, there is a registry of psychologists who have been licensed by their state and meet the minimum qualifications of the American Psychological Association for independent clinical practice.

A psychiatrist is a person who holds a medical degree (M.D. or D.O.) and has completed a residency in psychiatry, which is usually three years of study and clinical practice after receiving a medical degree. If they have completed all of the training necessary according to the certification procedures set down by a board in psychiatry and neurology they are "board eligible." Not all psychiatrists take the boards, but if they do and pass they are termed "board certified."

Psychologists, psychiatrists, and social workers can all perform interviewing, counseling, psychotherapy, consultation, and evaluation. Psychiatrists, however, are additionally qualified to prescribe drugs, since they possess a medical degree. The psychologist and social worker will get a physician in as a consultant if medicine needs to be prescribed.

The psychologist may also be involved in educational and personality testing. The social worker probably has the most training in and awareness of the use of social agencies and other community resources. All three professions have people who specialize further in such areas as psychoanalysis (an intensive form of therapy whose goal is personality change) and behavior therapy (an approach whose aim is modification of inappropriate, observable behavior).

There are naturally other professionals who are involved in helping others in emotional stress. These include pastoral counselors, psychiatric nurses, and mental health workers. For a description of their training and goals, the reader is referred to one of the books on entering psychotherapy listed in the bibliography.

It should be recognized that a license or a degree does not make a professional good. All that these do is certify that the person has passed a number of exams and fulfilled a number of stated qualifications. These qualifications have been set up for the public's protection, however. So although they don't guarantee anything, they reduce the chances that the person will be treated by someone who is unqualified. Accordingly, when someone goes to a practitioner of some type of therapy who is not recognized by some training body, that person is taking a chance. This is not to say that such people cannot be of help; it's just there is greater question as to whether or not they have received enough supervised training.

TYPES OF TREATMENT

Therapies seem to multiply like rabbits, and there seems to be new twists and approaches on the scene every year. Dr. Joel Kovel in his book *A Complete Guide to Therapy* presents an indepth description of the more widely known of the current approaches. Yet, despite the confusing array of techniques and philosophies presently in use, a majority of therapies seem to fall into one of the following categories: eclectic psychotherapy, behavior therapy, psychoanalysis, and drug therapy.

The eclectic psychotherapist borrows techniques from a

number of schools of thought. The main integrating force is the therapist's personality and background. Usually this type of therapy centers around the patient or client talking a good deal about what they feel and think in any situation which causes them problems. They are encouraged to bring in their fears, concerns, dreams, daydreams, conflicts, anxieties, joys, emotions, thoughts. In essence they are asked to sit back and let the information flow as it comes to mind.

The therapist then asks questions, interprets, reflects, and helps to clarify current issues under discussion. The focus is on anything the person brings up, but attention is usually given to interpersonal relations, styles of dealing with the world, and what is going on interpersonally between the therapist and the patient.

In behavior therapy there is an interest in dealing with the reported symptoms and signs which the person finds disabling. Though the relationship between therapist and client is important, the therapist is not interested in what can't be seen, which might be causing the problem (unconscious etiology), but wants to work with behaviors, which are by definition observable.

Psychoanalysis is only for those individuals who have good financial resources, a high verbal capability, and are intelligent. In addition, many analysts prefer to deal primarily with those patients not psychotic (persons often not in contact with reality), although, this is changing. Psychoanalysis requires a minimum of three sessions per week, it is costly in terms of money and time, and its effectiveness in all but certain cases is being seriously questioned today. However, in cases where it is designated as the "treatment of choice" and the person can afford the time and money, remarkable positive results are possible.

Drug therapy involves the use of psychotropic, mind altering, chemical substances, which are usually used as an adjunct to therapy. Some studies have shown, for instance, that an antipsychotic drug along with therapy is more effective than employing either the drugs or the therapy alone. (An antipsychotic drug, also known as a major tranquilizer, is used to reduce the occurrence of hallucinations, delusions, and social withdrawal.)

Antidepressant drugs are used with depressed people who are having difficulty responding to therapy alone, or with whom it appears that the primary cause of difficulty is chemical in origin. Within this classification can be included the drug lithium carbonate, which is used with people who suffer from manic depression and severe mood swings.

Another major category of drugs, are the minor tranquilizers or anti-anxiety agents. Possibly the most famous of these are Valium, Librium, and Miltown. They are prescribed by a physician for short periods of time to help a person deal with minor anxiety. In the therapy situation they may be prescribed for variable durations of time.

There is a good deal of danger in using the minor tranquilizers. Not only can they be harmful if used indiscriminatly in large amounts or in combination with alcohol or other drugs, but one can build up a tolerance to them. This means that larger and larger doses are required to get the same effect. Also, minor tranquilizers produce a physical dependence, and people find it hard to do without them. Thus their continued use, except under the supervision of a psychiatrist and in conjunction with therapy, is generally discouraged. Continual prescription by a family physician is not recommended.

Other drugs used therapeutically for people with emotional problems include hypnotics, sedatives, and stimulants. Many of these are listed in the accompanying chart.

The important thing to recognize is that in most cases, drug therapy alone will not alleviate the problem. Drugs are not a magical cure. They are designed to help a person get through an acute crisis or get to a point where he or she can utilize therapy to more permanently deal with the problem.

CONSUMERISM

A mental health expert, like any consultant, is paid to deliver a service. If the person you encourage to get help doesn't

PSYCHOTROPIC DRUGS

Antipsychotic Drugs

Use*: Control the symptoms of very disturbed persons (i.e., those categorized as psychotic); reduce hallucinations, delusions, and asocial behavior

Popular brands: Thorazine, Prolixin, Trilafon, Compazine, Sparine, Haldol, Navane, Lithane, Mellaril, Stelazine

Antianxiety Drugs

Use: Control anxiety; help individuals going through acute withdrawal from alcohol; relieve muscle spasms

Popular brands: Valium, Librium, Libritabs, Serax, Verstran, Tranxene, Miltown, Equanil, Atarax

Antidepressant Drugs

Use: Treat certain forms of depression; frequently employed in conjunction with psychotherapy, sometimes with electroconvulsive (shock) therapy

Popular brands: Elavil, Endep, Norpramin, Pertofrane, Adapin, Sinequan, Tofranil, Vivactil, Trilafon

Sedatives and Hypnotics

Use: Reduce excitability and motor activity; help for persons suffering from insomnia

Popular brands: Luminal, Amytal, Alurate, Butison, Lotusate, Phanodorn, Nembutal, Seconal, Sedamyl, Bromural, Beta-Chor, Dalmane, Doriden, Quaalude, Noludar, Paral, Triclos

Stimulants

Use: Treatment of obesity, hyperactivity in children, narcolepsy, mild depressive reactions

Popular brands: Benzedrine, Dexedrine, Dexoxyn, Ritalin, Cylert, Pondimin, Sanores, Voranil, Tepanil, Bacarate, Fastin, Wilpo

---

*Uses listed do not represent all current recommended medical uses.

believe he or she is getting it, then the therapist should be confronted with this fact. The negative feelings the person expresses may be simply resistence to treatment, but they may also be a result of legitimate dissatisfaction. So if people in therapy feel they are not being treated correctly, then they should say so.

There are a number of options open. First, they should bring their feelings to the therapist's attention and try to work it out. Often this step will get satisfactory results. If time is allotted to work the problem out and still nothing seems to improve, then a consultation with another professional might be in order. People who feel therapy is not proceeding appropriately can rightfully request such a consultation, and no respectable therapist would refuse to permit it. As a matter of fact, if they are baffled, they may request it themselves.

The final step which can be taken is termination of treatment with that therapist. This is a last resort and should only be done after carefully examining the situation. It's always helpful to ask the question: What is it about the therapist that bothers me now that didn't before? This should lead to a discovery as to whether it is the therapist who has changed and produced a negative response, or whether the person is getting close to something that scares him or her, but that should be worked through.

In line with good consumerism, the paying customer shouldn't be subjected to any treatment which is not in his or her best interest. The patient should not have to deal with a therapist who is frequently absent or late for sessions; have the confidentiality of the session breached; be treated in a sexist or prejudicial fashion because of one's race, color, creed, age, gender, or background; or have sex with the therapist.

The fact that a person is a therapist does not give him or her the right to exploit the client. Becoming a patient doesn't mean one gives up one's rights. Any therapist who doesn't show respect for an individual, lacks honesty, and displays exploitive behavior cannot be worth going to—it's as simple as that.

Chapter 12

Common Questions about Helping Others

When participating in small group discussions or giving lectures to members of civic organizations and college audiences, I am always asked a number of common questions about counseling and emotional distress. A sampling of them appears below. In some instances the material presented is a review of the concepts, techniques, and positions discussed in earlier chapters. Other answers contain information which complements, or builds upon, the material presented so far.

What you've said about our being able to help our family, friends, and those with whom we work sounds reasonable and you inspire me to do it. However, I still have a nagging doubt about the whole thing. Can an untrained, nontherapist REALLY do something to help others in distress?

It depends upon what you mean by "really do something." The nagging doubt may be tied to a number of things, and one of them is the expectations you have of yourself in working with others. It may be too high and quite unrealistic. As long as you recognize that you're not expected to provide a *cure* for the person in the form of a magical alleviation of symptoms, I think you will gain more confidence in the positive role you can play. Believe me, if a depressed neighbor or a coworker under stress has someone like you to talk to who will be accepting, supportive, willing to listen, and interested enough to begin problem solving with them, your presence as a helper can make all the difference.

The other point I want to make regarding your reluctance is that professionals have long resisted the entry of nonprofessionals into the mental health arena. This is now changing. We now realize that preventive psychiatry and community psychology cannot work unless we all become involved. Consequently, there is a push now to eliminate the myths surrounding stress, depression, anxiety, and so-called bizzare behavior.

I must admit I'm a bit afraid of talking to someone who is having a problem. I worry that I'll say the wrong thing and the person will blow up or get more upset. Is there anything I can do about this feeling?

Recognizing where your hesitation is coming from is probably the biggest step you might take in an effort to deal with it. The fear you have is an irrational one which is shared by all new professional counselors and therapists. The unreasonable thought is: If I say something right, the person will be cured; if I don't, he'll have a nervous breakdown right here in front of me.

This thought is understandable because most people are nervous when they reach out to others who are undergoing emotional upheavals. Yet, it is not precisely *what* you say that makes the most impact, but the fact that you're taking out the time and effort to say something, or silently listen to the other person's difficulty. Through your warm accepting approach you can help someone. Even if you say something very foolish or provocative and the person seems upset over it, the person will probably overlook it; considering your generally helpful stance. And if they do get upset, then wait it out and deal with it. You're human, entitled to make mistakes, and the person you're dealing with is more resilient than you imagine.

Remember this, the person in need is better off having a friend who will reach out to him or her and risk saying something which might not be terribly smart or helpful, than having an acquaintance who for fear of getting into an unpleasant situation, runs away and avoids the responsibility of friendship.

I've read a bit on counseling and I've listened to the techniques and principles you've expounded on here. The problem is I can't seem to remember them when working with the people I supervise who come to me with difficulties. So, what I finally do is say the heck with it and just be myself.

Counseling and interviewing techniques are not designed to stifle your personal talents and style of dealing with others, they are meant to extend them more effectively. If people keep coming to you for interpersonal support, then you're probably an easy person to talk to. The point is to try to incorporate those techniques you hear and read about which fit in with your style.

This can be done in a couple of ways. The first is by so-called over-learning. By reading and re-reading a basic counseling and interviewing primer, you will soon be able to organize the principles in such a way that they will come to mind without too much effort. The second is by looking at the counseling material and trying to see how the material can be applied in a practical way to your own situation, and the specific people you deal with.

If you've had, and still have, problems yourself, how can you be of help to someone else?

Having problems does not disqualify someone from being an understanding, helpful individual with another person experiencing difficulties. As a matter of fact, people who have experienced similar problems can often be of particular help to others undergoing unpleasant occurrences in life. The helper does not

have to have conquered his own problem. Just sharing with
someone one's desire to try to work things out can be motivating. We see this in self-help groups like Alcoholics Anonymous
and Recovery (a group of people who have experienced emotional distress). One of the few possible drawbacks may be that,
if your are experiencing problems yourself, working with someone with a similar, or seemingly overwhelming problem may be
too much to handle at that time. Some people undergoing
certain forms of depression, for example, feel that being with
others who are down is too disturbing for them. In this instance, helping another person in a similar situation might be
best put off, but this is an exception rather than a general rule
of thumb.

*Anytime I think of myself as a helper, I think of a friend of mine
and I get turned off to doing it. He has a B.A. in psychology and is
as obnoxious as hell in the way he interprets everything and analyzes
people. I certainly don't want to be like him.*

You don't have to be and you shouldn't be. A helper doesn't
try to inflate his or her own ego at the expense of the person in
distress. Moreover, reaching out to other people doesn't include lauding over them and using all kinds of unproductive
intellectual devices and games. People who do that are usually
somewhat immature and defensive themselves. There's a big
difference between being a warm listener and being a know-it-
all advice giver. I guess a little knowledge can be a dangerous
thing for some people, particularly those who think in terms of
power and control of others, rather than in terms of generosity.

*You say that the use of silence is important in counseling others,
but I feel foolish being silent when someone has come to me for help.
If someone asks me for help I feel like I'm letting the person down or
ignoring him if I don't say anything.*

When people come to you for specific details about some
issue, it would be inappropriate to respond by saying nothing.
This is often not the case though. People in trouble usually

come to pour their hearts out and be heard out. Even if they ask a question, it usually is best answered with a question and followed by a silent period. This is not a ploy so you won't have to give your opinion, but rather a means to help clarify the feelings and meaning of the question further and to get the person to look more closely at his or her own concerns and thoughts about the issue in question. In counseling we believe that being a sounding board rather than an advice dispenser is more valuable and appropriate in most instances . . . and also more difficult.

I've read a bit about nonverbal communication in a couple of popular magazines. It sounds like a lot of baloney to me. I know I couldn't use it, but maybe I should. What do you think?

I think you probably use it already, but don't realize it. If you compare your commonsense use of nonverbal communication with the extravagant claims and training regimens offered by some authors, it may not seem that way, but you do.

Every time you look at a person's expression, take note of his or her voice rising, or get an awareness that someone seems uptight or relaxed, you are noting and employing nonverbal communication to understand and deal with other people and their behavior. The point to make about nonverbal communication is that the more you know about it, and about how you use it, the more you can monitor it for your own benefit.

I'd like to help people, but I don't want to be nosey by asking a lot of questions that I have no business knowing. In helping people, how do I know how far to go in what I ask?

Ask as few questions as possible is the general rule. And when you ask something, it should be only in reference to what the person is discussing. If he or she brings up the topic, it's open game, though naturally the person may refuse to answer something even though the topic was originally brought up by them. Curiosity for curiosity's sake should not be present in a helping relationship—be it professional or otherwise. When a question is asked, it is because the answer may shed light on the problem at hand; if it can't help in some direct way, then it shouldn't be brought up.

Can I really help my husband, daughter, or close friend if the problem relates directly to me?

When you're directly involved, there are many limitations to trying to help someone else. For example, if you are the person your husband is mad at, trying to counsel him would probably cause more problems than it would alleviate. He might think you were patronizing or trying to shift the blame. However using counseling principles in trying to get to the bottom of the situation may be quite helpful. For instance, active listening and problem solving may help you find out what the problem is in more detail and how the two of you can work on it more productively.

I try to be of help to friends who seem to be having problems, but they don't listen. They just do the same thing over and over. It's no wonder they have difficulties. This gets me annoyed and I wonder why I should bother with them?

The problematic styles people use in dealing with the world usually have developed over a number of years, so they're not going to change over night—even if they say they want to and vow to do so. When people reach out for help we have to realize this or, as you say, it can be really frustrating.

One of the traits of a good helper is patience. In working with others, we must allow for people to do the same thing over and over again, even if it does get them into trouble. If we are able to stick with them, though, and not be tricked into preaching because they appear to want us to lecture them on how to mend their ways, their lives will be better for it. Remember, our goal is not to change them, but to accept them, allow them to be themselves, and help them see where they are in life. If they want to change something, they decide; we don't.

Everytime she has a problem, my neighbor gets teary eyed. She seems like such a baby, I feel like telling her to bite the bullet. A lot of people are in worse situations than she is. Still, I feel sorry for her and would like to be of help. What can I do?

One thing that might help you to work with her is to recognize and accept her style of dealing with stress. Her childlike behavior is a style of facing unpleasant, anxiety-provoking situations, as are hostility, depression, withdrawal, denial, and false courage.

If you can view her style in this way, you may in time become more patient with her. If you can do this it may be extremely helpful for her. Not only can she have someone to turn to who won't turn her away, but someone who might in time be able to help her see how her style might be adversely affecting other people and situations she claims she is interested in pursuing. However, the important thing is patience, for if she has someone like you to depend on, it may mean all the world to her and give her the needed support to progress rather than regress.

In working with people who have problems, I feel like I'm picking on them. They tell me what they've done and I point out how they messed it up and should change. It leaves me with an uncomfortable feeling, even though as a supervisor I need to help them deal with their limitations.

In interviewing, we try to elicit a pattern of the person's assets, as well as his or her liabilities. In counseling, we try to help them emphasize and utilize their talents in a more effective way. So in helping others we are not just on a pathology/personal faults hunt, we are trying to point to what abilities they have as well. Therefore, if you see counseling in this light and this philosophy comes across, you should not only feel better about what you are doing, but your efforts will turn out to be more effective.

My brother will come over to visit and talk about problems on the job. I feel so helpless. He'll start to get into it and then say he's

*sorry he's bothering me with it, that since I don't know the ins and
outs of his business, he's probably wasting my time and his and he
leaves. I find this is a problem with many people who come to me as a
friend or family member; I just don't know enough about the specifics
to be of help.*

To help people you need to get enough details to get an idea
of what's involved in the situation they're having problems
with. In the case of your brother the situation is his job.
However, you don't need to know the business inside and out.
As a helper, you're a consultant to the person and his problems—which are probably interpersonal in nature. The difficulties he's probably having are with *people,* not policies or business
systems. They may be part of it, and this part can be quickly
explained to you. But most of his difficulties probably concern
the people who make the policies and operate the business
systems, and in this area you can be of help, if he lets you.

Indicate this to him. Show your patience by listening carefully, and try to encourage him to continue. He may not go on
and explain further for other reasons (he may feel you *will*
understand all too well and criticize or chastise him), but he also
may surprise you and continue.

*Counselors generally don't give advice. They give feedback.
What's the difference?*

Advice is telling people what to do. It is giving information
from our vantage point. Feedback is providing our impression
of what *they* have been saying verbally and nonverbally to see if
they agree with our impressions. What this does is allow people
to see someone else's impression of how they (the counselees)
feel, think about, and have been handling a problem and the
alternatives open to them.

Feedback is essentially a reflection process. In giving feedback, we are trying to act as a mirror to get them to see better
where they stand and the options open to them.

The timing of feedback is also important. People will often

give you a small portion of information and ask you what you think. Your aim at this point is to try to elicit more material through open questioning and reflection of their feelings. This is essential because providing feedback is easier and more useful when it is a summary of their answers to questions and their full discussion of alternatives than when it is given with only a little bit of data in hand.

My cousin seems uptight all of the time. How do I determine whether she needs professional help?

You have done it already. If she is uptight *all the time* and has taken steps to correct the situation, then she probably could use at least an evaluation of the problem. In trying to assess whether or not people need professional help, remember some of the questions we should ask: How serious is the problem in terms of duration and degree? Is the problem interfering with her daily functioning to a degree where she and others readily notice it? Has she sought to alleviate the problem through personal reflection, help from friends, and normal family supports (e.g., clergy, physician, etc.)?

How useful or harmful are drugs in the treatment of emotional problems?

Drug therapy, as an adjunct to other kinds of therapy, can be particularly helpful when used with temporary problems or with severe or chronic problems that indicate a need for chemotherapy. However, many factors affect the usefulness or potential harm of using drugs to treat emotional problems. One difficulty which may arise is if a physician in general or family practice prescribes a psychotropic drug on a long-term basis without getting a psychological or psychiatric consultation. Another problem may arise if the physician does not take into account the patient's use of other drugs, including alcohol, when prescribing psychotropic drugs.

Still another problem is when drugs are used strictly for control purposes, for example, when a patient in a hospital is given massive doses of drugs to prevent aggressive behavior.

A final point to note is that when drugs are employed on a long-term basis, they are usually used as an adjunct to therapy. In some cases where it is believed that there is a biochemical basis to depression, drug therapy is primary and little if any psychological therapy is provided, but this approach is used only in certain cases and is considered questionable by some mental health professionals.

Is Valium dangerous? So many people seem to be taking it.

Valium and other anti-anxiety agents are generally safe when used as directed. The problem arises when people use it in conjunction with other drugs or alcohol, or do not follow the schedule of usage prescribed by the physician.

The good thing about anti-anxiety drugs like Valium is that they produce virtually no side effects as do the antipsychotic drugs. However, they can be harmful when taken in great quantities (overdose), when people become dependent upon them, and when people develop a tolerance to them, thus requiring increasingly larger doses to obtain the same therapeutic effect. This is why long-term use of them is usually only recommended when the person is also in therapy with a psychologist, psychiatrist, social worker, or other mental health professional.

The important thing is that any psychotropic drug should be used not as a crutch, but only when necessary. Also, when someone needs a drug, a medical consultation should be sought with a physician initially, and with a psychiatrist if long-term use is indicated.

If someone needs to be on drugs, then, do they have to be in therapy with a psychiatrist?

No. Psychologists and other nonmedical therapists usually have a psychiatrist who they use as a medical consultant. The psychologist will send the patient to a psychiatrist for a medical evaluation and to see the patient periodically as long as he or she is on the medication.

The three most common psychiatric labels I've heard are "neurotic," "psychotic," and "psychopath." What's the difference between them?

There are many labels used in psychiatric and psychological classification schemas. While we use them for guidance, using them can often lead to problems since they are so general they often do not exactly fit the people to whom they are applied.

A "neurotic" is generally seen as someone who is functioning in the world on a day-to-day basis, but not doing it well. The person is using conscious coping mechanisms and unconscious defense mechanisms to ward off the anxiety being felt as a result of great conflict. This kind of person we can generally see as having problems in daily life. We recognize that we use similar methods of avoiding or dealing with stress and guilt, but their use of such mechanisms (anger or denial, for example) is quite exaggerated.

A "psychotic" is someone who often is not in touch with reality. This category is generally reserved for the very emotionally disturbed who have such symptoms and signs as hallucinations, delusions, agitation, extreme apathy, and very serious problems with regard to mood or their ability to formulate logical, reality-based lines of thought.

The "psychopath" is a person who has poor impulse control, does not experience a normal amount of guilt when committing antisocial acts, does not like to postpone anything that provides pleasure, is unable to form lasting give-and-take relationships, and does not usually learn from punishment.

Are mentally ill people dangerous?

A very, very small portion of the people we label as mentally ill are dangerous. Some psychotic individuals may seem dangerous because their bizarre behavior is strange to us, but the portion of people who are emotionally disturbed that are also potentially dangerous is extremely small.

You hear a lot about middle-age crises. Is it easy for a seemingly confident man in his forties to get thrown into turmoil by a crisis at that age?

As you might expect, it depends upon a number of factors, including the personality of the man, the type of crisis, and the supports and resources he can call upon in his family and the extended community.

If the combinations are correct, a person whom you might least expect can be really thrown into a helpless position quite easily. For instance, a seemingly confident and successful executive loses his position because of a merger. If his whole identity and self-esteem were attached to the position, and he had been growing apart from his family and friends, he might find it quite difficult to cope.

Are the self-help and pop-psychology books really useless trash? I get the feeling I'm being taken over the coals when I buy a book in the psychology/psychiatry section of my bookstore.

Given all of the sensational and poorly documented material on the market, I'm not surprised you feel that way. However, there are some excellent books on psychological topics. There are several fine medical and psychological writers who on their own, or in collaboration with mental health professionals, are presenting important recent findings in mental health.

Some of the works out now on behavior therapy, transactional analysis, personality, and aggression bear this out. Yet, as you indicate, it is difficult to weed them out when there is such a large group of books which at best are psychological pablum. Care in the selection can make all the difference.

In selecting a psychology book which I can understand, is it better, then, to pick one written solely by a professional?

Not necessarily. Professionals can get off on unscientific tangents as well. Having an M.D. or Ph.D. sell some message of fulfillment is not unusual today. On the other hand, good books written by professional writers familiar with the behavioral sciences are also on the market. In many cases, because the professional writers resemble the public they are writing for, they ask more practical questions in researching the topics, and their style of presentation may make the books more interesting and easier to follow. The problem arises when the writer is only interested in making money and sensationalizing a topic with the goal of just selling books. But many mental health professionals are guilty of this, as well.

Isn't going into therapy seen by many as a sign of weakness?

Yes, and the existence of this feeling in this modern era is surprising. If a person with a Mercedes called in a mechanic to look at his car or someone with a growth on his arm went to a medical specialist, no one would think anything further. It's logical to get a professional consultant when a problem is perplexing and beyond our range of knowledge.

Yet, given the stigma attached to getting mental health assistance, and the myth that everyone should naturally be able to handle *every* personal crisis that comes up, some people think obtaining a mental health consultation is a sign of weakness. Thank goodness this outlook is changing. People are beginning to see therapy as a facilitating process. And they are starting to take note of the fact that very talented people are sometimes involved in therapy when their growth is impeded by some issue which they are having a continual problem resolving.

On another front, therapy is also being seen in light of its real limitations. No longer are people flocking to therapy for every little issue, or as the one true road to happiness and success.

What prejudices should a person in therapy look out for when starting the process?

Once a therapist is selected, the patient should be alert to any prejudice which might interfere with the treatment. Therapists

are people, and like any group of people, there are some who
are biased in one way or another due to issues in age, sex, race,
creed, style of living, etc. If a therapist seems intent on controlling the client and inflicting his or her own philosophy of life on
the client, this should be brought out. Likewise, when
therapists make comments which show strong leanings which
interfere with treatment (i.e. chauvinistic tendencies, bias
against older persons), they should be confronted with this to
see if it is in fact the case.

*Lately, the therapy I've been hearing about is sex therapy? What
is it?*

Sex therapy is defined in different ways by different therapists. Generally however, sex therapy's goal is usually directed
at helping people who are having problems with their sex life.
This may include impotency, frigidity, premature ejaculation,
and other problems related to sexual relations. In most types
of sex therapy, interpersonal issues as well as ones dealing directly with sexual acts are dealt with. Sex therapy can be obtained from private practioners and in clinic settings in most
urban areas.

*Isn't it true that most therapists don't really care for their clients,
but just see them because they get paid?*

Just because a person gets paid for conducting therapy
doesn't mean he or she doesn't care. Caring and getting reimbursement for treatment aren't mutually exclusive elements.
Conversely, people who don't get paid for listening don't necessarily have to have the person's best interest at heart. It's true,
some therapists don't care what happens to their clients. To
deny this would be to deny the variances in humanity, but to
make a generalization that therapists don't care would be
wrong. As a matter of fact, in general I have found it to be the
opposite. Therapists care more than the clients ever know.

People are always coming to me for help. I enjoy listening to them and being supportive. Is there anyting I can do to improve my style?

Continue to read books and articles on counseling, human development, the psychology of adjustment and other areas of applied psychology. This will help you to better understand yourself, other people, and how to help them. Also, reviewing how you handled something after a person has left is very useful. Sometimes doing this with a confidante who will not divulge what you have discussed can be invaluable. In such instances, though, you have to be careful that this person will keep everything you discuss confidential; otherwise, your actions will be unethical since people expect their secrets to remain secret.

However, if people are coming to you again and again for help at home or at work, you have already taken the most important step in helping others. You have successfully demonstrated that you are willing and able to reach out to others in need—a not so small thing in these times of hustle and bustle, isolation, and selfishness.

Index

Acceptance, showing of, 100, 101
Active listening, 13
Alcohol abuse, 138-141
   complications of, 139, 140
   and depressive behavior, 140
   symptoms of, 139, 140
Alternatives, opening up, 75-81
Amphetamine abuse, 143
Anger, 5
   and depression, 117-121
   displacement of, 57
Antianxiety drugs, 187
Antidepressant drugs, 186, 187
Antipsychotic drugs, 187
Anxiety, 7, 121-128
   causes of, 123, 124
   coping with, 124, 125
   in daily life, 121-123
   getting caught up in
      another's, 126-128
   too little of, 123
   too much of, 123, 124

Anxious people, 125
   counseling of, 125-128
Assault, 146-148
Assets, focusing on, 67-69

"Bad trips," 141, 142
Behaviors, pointing out of, 96, 97
Behavior therapy, 185
Biases and prejudices, 47-50
   negative, 47
   positive, 48
Bizarre behavior, 144-146
Body language, 13-16
Brainstorming, 78, 86, 87

Caplan, Dr. Gerald, 150
Change, 101, 102, 128
Childlike behavior (*see:*
   defensive styles)
Clarifying issues, 69-75

Communication, 7
  block to, 7, 8
Consumerism, 186, 188
Conversation, 21, 22. (*see also:*
  interview)
Counseling
  of anxious people, 125-128
  and clarification of issues, 69-75
  definition of, 62
  as distinct from therapy, 61, 62
  and exploration of
    feelings, 62-67
  and focusing on assets, 67-69
  goals of, 61-81
  guidelines for, 89-103
  and the opening up of
    alternatives, 75-81
  and the reflection of
    emotions, 65-67
  tips, 93
Crisis intervention, 133-155
  and divorce, 152-155
  an illustration of, 152

Defense mechanisms, 125, 172
Defensive styles, 51-60
  and childlike behavior, 54-56
  and denial, 51-54
  and depression, 56, 57, 59
  and evasion, 58, 59
  and false courage, 51-54
  and hostility, 56, 57
Delirium tremens, 140
Delusions, 173
Denial (*see:* defensive styles)
Depression, 104-121
  and anger, 117-121
  in children and
    adolescents, 105, 106
  and helplessness, 110-117
  physical causes of, 109, 110

  psychological causes of,
    110-117
  signs of, 106-109
Displacement, 125
DMT (dimenthylbyplamine), 141
DOM (dimethoxymethylam-
    phetamine), 141
Drug abuse, 138-145
  (*see also:* specific drug listings)
Drugs, types of, 186, 187
Drug therapy, 185, 186

Emergencies (*see also:* crisis
    intervention)
  mental health, 133
  self-injurious behavior, 134-138
Emotions, exploring, 62-67
Evaluating the problem, 101, 102
Evasion (*see:* defensive styles)

Facial expressions, interpretation
  of, 16, 17
False courage (*see:*
    defensive styles)
Feedback, 99, 100
Feelings, exploring, 62-67
Frame of reference, 44-47

Generalizations, questioning
  of, 97-99
Goals of counseling, 61-81
Guidelines for counseling, 89-103

Hallucinations, 173
Hallucinogens, 141, 142
Helper, distorted view of, 50, 51
Helping others, common
  questions about, 189-203

Helplessness, 37, 57, 110-117
Hofmann, Albert, 141
Hopelessness, 57, 70
Hostility (*see:* defensive styles)
Humility, 24, 25
Hypnotics, 187

Information, gathering of, 21-44
Interview, 82-88
   initial opening in, 82, 83
   key clues in, 83, 84
   stages of the, 82-88
   unburdening in, 83, 84
Interviewing, 21-44

Life crises, 151
Listening, 6-20
LSD (d-lysergic acid
      diethylamide), 141

Mental health
   crises, 133
   emergency, 133
   evaluation, 179
   workers, 182-184
Modeling problem-solving
      behavior, 55-56

Neurosis, 125
Neurotic, 199
   behavior, 172
Nonverbal signs, 13-20
   recognition in others, 13-16
   recognition in self, 17-20

Opiate overdose, 142, 143
Overdose (*see:* drug abuse)

Pacing, 93, 94
Parent, playing of, 23
Patience, 102, 103
Personality, 29
Pop-psychology (*see:* self-help)
Prejudices (*see:* biases)
Problem solving, 75-81, 99, 100
Professional help, 169-188
   and consumerism, 186, 188
   how to suggest it, 176
   the need for, 171
Psychoanalysis, 185
Psychopath, 199
Psychotherapy, 182-186
Psychotic, 199
Psychotropic drugs, 187
Purposeful conversation, 22

Questioning, 25-41
   the art of, 25-28
   getting details of complaint,
      34-37
   and interruptions, 28
   principles of, 25-28
Questions
   about helping others, 189-203
   answering questions with,
      37-40
   focus of, 29-32
   level of, 33, 34
   types of, 26-28

Rape, 148-150
Rationalization, 125, 172
Reaction formation, 53
Reactions, criticism of our
      own, 47-50
Reflection
   as a counseling technique,
      90-92
   process of, 65-68

Responses, dealing with
  unsatisfactory, 41

Sadness, 104-105
Saviour complex, 8-10, 11, 16
Sedatives, 187
Self-help and pop-psychology
    books, 165-168
  advantages of, 164-166
  the appeal of, 157-160
  limitations of, 160-164
  selection, use, and
    recommendation of, 166-168
Self-injurious behavior (SIB),
    134-138
Self-reflection, 91, 92
Sex therapy, 202
Silence, 10-12
Specifics, dealing with, 95, 96
Stimulants, 187

Stress, 128-132
  basic source of, 128
  causes of, 128-130
  handling of, 128-132
  manifestation of, 129
Suicide, 134-137
Suppression, 172

Therapy, 180-186
  ground rules of, 180, 181
  types of treatment in, 184-186
Tranquilizers, 186, 187
Transitions between topics, 41-43

Understanding, and tuning into
  others, 44-59

Williams, Paul, 13